OPPOSING VIEWPOINTS® SERIES

| Sanctuary Cities

Other Books of Related Interest

Opposing Viewpoints Series
Illegal Immigration
Immigration Bans
Western Democracy at Risk

At Issue Series
Civil Disobedience
Domestic Terrorism
Immigration Reform

Current Controversies Series
Are There Two Americas?
The Border Wall with Mexico
Deporting Immigrants

"Congress shall make
no law ... abridging
the freedom of speech,
or of the press."

First Amendment to the US Constitution

The basic foundation of our democracy is the First Amendment guarantee of freedom of expression. The Opposing Viewpoints series is dedicated to the concept of this basic freedom and the idea that it is more important to practice it than to enshrine it.

OPPOSING
VIEWPOINTS®
SERIES

Sanctuary Cities

Marcia Amidon Lusted, Book Editor

GREENHAVEN
PUBLISHING

Published in 2019 by Greenhaven Publishing, LLC
353 3rd Avenue, Suite 255, New York, NY 10010

Cover image: Ronen Tivony/NurPhoto via Getty Images

Library of Congress Cataloging-in-Publication Data

Names: Lusted, Marcia Amidon, editor.
Title: Sanctuary cities / Marcia Amidon Lusted, book editor.
Description: First edition. | New York : Greenhaven Publishing, 2019. |
  Series: Opposing viewpoints | Includes bibliographical references and
  index. | Audience: Grade 9 to 12.
Identifiers: LCCN 2018000430| ISBN 9781534502994 (library bound) | ISBN
  9781534503007 (pbk.)
Subjects: LCSH: Illegal aliens—Government policy—United States—Juvenile
  literature. | United States—Emigration and immigration—Government
  policy—Juvenile literature. | Urban policy—United States—Juvenile
  literature. | Central-local government relations—United States—Juvenile
  literature.
Classification: LCC JV6483 .S27 2019 | DDC 325.73—dc23
LC record available at https://lccn.loc.gov/2018000430

Manufactured in the United States of America

Website: http://greenhavenpublishing.com

Contents

Chapter 1: Whom Do Sanctuary Cities Protect?

Chapter 2: Are Crime Rates Higher in Sanctuary Cities?

Chapter 3: Do Sanctuary Cities Undermine National Security?

Chapter 4: Do Sanctuary Cities Help to Maintain Democracy?

The Importance of Opposing Viewpoints

Perhaps every generation experiences a period in time in which the populace seems especially polarized, starkly divided on the important issues of the day and gravitating toward the far ends of the political spectrum and away from a consensus-facilitating middle ground. The world that today's students are growing up in and that they will soon enter into as active and engaged citizens is deeply fragmented in just this way. Issues relating to terrorism, immigration, women's rights, minority rights, race relations, health care, taxation, wealth and poverty, the environment, policing, military intervention, the proper role of government—in some ways, perennial issues that are freshly and uniquely urgent and vital with each new generation—are currently roiling the world.

If we are to foster a knowledgeable, responsible, active, and engaged citizenry among today's youth, we must provide them with the intellectual, interpretive, and critical-thinking tools and experience necessary to make sense of the world around them and of the all-important debates and arguments that inform it. After all, the outcome of these debates will in large measure determine the future course, prospects, and outcomes of the world and its peoples, particularly its youth. If they are to become successful members of society and productive and informed citizens, students need to learn how to evaluate the strengths and weaknesses of someone else's arguments, how to sift fact from opinion and fallacy, and how to test the relative merits and validity of their own opinions against the known facts and the best possible available information. The landmark series Opposing Viewpoints has been providing students with just such critical-thinking skills and exposure to the debates surrounding society's most urgent contemporary issues for many years, and it continues to serve this essential role with undiminished commitment, care, and rigor.

The key to the series' success in achieving its goal of sharpening students' critical-thinking and analytic skills resides in its title—

Opposing Viewpoints. In every intriguing, compelling, and engaging volume of this series, readers are presented with the widest possible spectrum of distinct viewpoints, expert opinions, and informed argumentation and commentary, supplied by some of today's leading academics, thinkers, analysts, politicians, policy makers, economists, activists, change agents, and advocates. Every opinion and argument anthologized here is presented objectively and accorded respect. There is no editorializing in any introductory text or in the arrangement and order of the pieces. No piece is included as a "straw man," an easy ideological target for cheap point-scoring. As wide and inclusive a range of viewpoints as possible is offered, with no privileging of one particular political ideology or cultural perspective over another. It is left to each individual reader to evaluate the relative merits of each argument— as he or she sees it, and with the use of ever-growing critical-thinking skills—and grapple with his or her own assumptions, beliefs, and perspectives to determine how convincing or successful any given argument is and how the reader's own stance on the issue may be modified or altered in response to it.

This process is facilitated and supported by volume, chapter, and selection introductions that provide readers with the essential context they need to begin engaging with the spotlighted issues, with the debates surrounding them, and with their own perhaps shifting or nascent opinions on them. In addition, guided reading and discussion questions encourage readers to determine the authors' point of view and purpose, interrogate and analyze the various arguments and their rhetoric and structure, evaluate the arguments' strengths and weaknesses, test their claims against available facts and evidence, judge the validity of the reasoning, and bring into clearer, sharper focus the reader's own beliefs and conclusions and how they may differ from or align with those in the collection or those of their classmates.

Research has shown that reading comprehension skills improve dramatically when students are provided with compelling, intriguing, and relevant "discussable" texts. The subject matter of these collections could not be more compelling, intriguing, or urgently relevant to today's students and the world they are poised to inherit. The anthologized articles and the reading and discussion questions that are included with them also provide the basis for stimulating, lively, and passionate classroom debates. Students who are compelled to anticipate objections to their own argument and identify the flaws in those of an opponent read more carefully, think more critically, and steep themselves in relevant context, facts, and information more thoroughly. In short, using discussable text of the kind provided by every single volume in the Opposing Viewpoints series encourages close reading, facilitates reading comprehension, fosters research, strengthens critical thinking, and greatly enlivens and energizes classroom discussion and participation. The entire learning process is deepened, extended, and strengthened.

For all of these reasons, Opposing Viewpoints continues to be exactly the right resource at exactly the right time—when we most need to provide readers with the critical-thinking tools and skills that will not only serve them well in school but also in their careers and their daily lives as decision-making family members, community members, and citizens. This series encourages respectful engagement with and analysis of opposing viewpoints and fosters a resulting increase in the strength and rigor of one's own opinions and stances. As such, it helps make readers "future ready," and that readiness will pay rich dividends for the readers themselves, for the citizenry, for our society, and for the world at large.

Introduction

> *"Sanctuary cities were a critical victory won by activists. They were implemented because outraged immigrant communities—with assistance from federal courts that found detentions raised serious constitutional issues—successfully pressured cities to refuse to cooperate with federal detainer requests."*
>
> *Daniel Denvir,* Slate,
> *February 17, 2017*

On January 25, 2017, in his first week in office as president of the United States, Donald Trump signed an executive order entitled "Enhancing Public Safety in the Interior of the United States." It read, in part:

> Sanctuary jurisdictions across the United States willfully violate Federal law in an attempt to shield aliens from removal from the United States. These jurisdictions have caused immeasurable harm to the American people and to the very fabric of our Republic.[1]

The executive order went on to say:

> In furtherance of this policy, the Attorney General and the Secretary, in their discretion and to the extent consistent with law, shall ensure that jurisdictions that willfully refuse to comply with 8 U.S.C. 1373 (sanctuary jurisdictions) are not eligible to receive Federal grants, except as deemed necessary for law enforcement purposes by the Attorney General or the Secretary.[2]

President Trump's executive order was followed by another on January 27, entitled "Protecting the Nation from Foreign Terrorist Entry into the United States." It specified countries whose citizens would be prevented from entering the United States, in the interests of combating terrorism. It barred admission to the United States for anyone from Iraq, Iran, Libya, Somalia, Sudan, Syria and Yemen, even if they possessed valid visas.

The executive orders concerning immigration and sanctuary cities created a great deal of controversy. It also left people wondering just what a sanctuary city as, whether it was legal, and if it was in the best interests of American citizens that these cities existed. A sanctuary city does not have a specific definition, because it varies from state to state. But in general, it refers to a town or city that has enacted policies or laws that limit the extent to which its local law enforcement officials will cooperate with and assist federal immigration officials on immigration issues. According to the Congressional Research Service, the term *sanctuary city* "is often used to refer to those localities which, as a result of a state or local act, ordinance, policy, or fiscal constraints, place limits on their assistance to federal immigration authorities seeking to apprehend and remove unauthorized aliens."[3] By March of 2017, there were an estimated 500 cities and towns in the United States that had declared themselves to be sanctuary cities.

The controversy about these places comes from a sharp divide between supporters, who feel that sanctuary cities are in the spirit of democracy, and critics, who believe that these cities are offering safe havens for illegal aliens, especially those with criminal records or terrorist agendas. Sanctuary city advocates point to statistics that indicate less crime in these places because illegal immigrants do not fear deportation in reporting crimes to the local police. Critics point to incidents of violence and murder carried out by illegal immigrants and insist that keeping illegal aliens out of cities will reduce the creation of illegal schemes such as drug cartels, gang activity, and terrorist cells. When it comes to President Trump's threat to cut off federal funding to sanctuary cities, these cities argue that programs such as Medicare and other federal health programs, which serve US citizens, would also be affected.

Overall, many Americans do not even understand the issue of sanctuary cities, and fear that it will lead to a victimization of law-abiding US citizens. Supporters are quick to point out that it is only laws concerning illegal immigrants and undocumented persons that sanctuary cities are refusing to enforce. All other criminal laws are still enforced against these people.

As of December 2017, a federal judge had blocked President Trump's order to withhold federal grants and funding from sanctuary cities. However, the issue of illegal immigrants, deportation, and sanctuary cities continues to rage. Texas lawmakers passed a bill that banned sanctuary cities within the state, although a judge later temporarily blocked the ban. Other states are seeing a steady increase in the number of towns and cities that are declaring themselves as sanctuary cities, even when they are located in places where illegal immigrants are rare. It is a debate that will continue until permanent legislation makes a decision for or against the existence of sanctuary cities.

The viewpoints in *Opposing Viewpoints: Sanctuary Cities* grapple with these complex issues. A panel of scholars and professionals offer diverse perspectives in chapters titled "Whom Do Sanctuary Cities Protect?" "Are Crime Rates Higher in Sanctuary Cities?" "Do Sanctuary Cities Undermine National Security?" and "Do Sanctuary Cities Help Maintain Democracy?"

Endnotes

1. "Executive Order: Enhancing Public Safety in the Interior of the United States." The White House, January 25, 2017. Web. https://www.whitehouse.gov/presidential-actions/executive-order-enhancing-public-safety-interior-united-states/

2. "Executive Order: Enhancing Public Safety in the Interior of the United States."

3. Garcia, Michael John. "'Sanctuary Cities': Legal Issues." Congressional Research Service, January 15, 2009. Web. http://www.ilw.com/immigrationdaily/news/2011,0106-crs.pdf

OPPOSING VIEWPOINTS® SERIES

CHAPTER 1

Whom Do Sanctuary Cities Protect?

Chapter Preface

S anctuary cities have received a lot of media attention since the inauguration of President Donald Trump in January 2017. Trump campaigned on a promise to protect American citizens from terrorism and other negative situations that are believed to stem from illegal immigration. As a result, many cities began declaring themselves as sanctuary cities, places where immigrants could be protected from what were seen as unfair immigration policies. These cities also wanted to protect undocumented immigrants who had established roots and started families in the US, but were facing deportation as a result of new policies. These cities also wanted to ensure that immigrants would report crimes without fear of discovery and deportation, and enable them to become part of their communities.

The sanctuary cities movement is not new, however. The first where established in Northern cities during the Civil War, with the purpose of protecting fugitive slaves. In the 1980s, with the advent of protests against federal immigration policies that denied asylum to refugees from El Salvador and Guatemala, San Francisco passed a city ordinance that forbid its police force and city magistrates from assisting federal immigration authorities who might be detaining or deporting refugees from the city. More cities followed throughout the presidencies of George W. Bush and Barack Obama, as restrictive immigration policies affected other refugees.

The main issue in protecting undocumented and illegal immigrants is the fear of a rise in crime from immigrants who may have criminal records and haven't been vetted by the usual immigration policies. There is also a fear of terrorism. This is balanced against the determination of sanctuary cities to protect immigrants who have become part of their town or city and deserve to remain there, rather than being detained and deported according to the strict letter of immigration law.

| "Immigration policy has become increasingly fragmented across the country, with states enacting individual laws that reflect their own political, demographic, and ideological landscapes."

Local Law Enforcement Is Critical to Cracking Down on Illegal Immigration

Police Executive Research Forum

In the following excerpted viewpoint, authors at the Police Executive Research Forum reveal the results of a round table discussion between federal law enforcement officials and police officers from seven states, concerning the immigration policies in their states. The immigration laws in these states are detailed, whether strict or moderate, as well as the effects that these laws have had on law enforcement and immigration in those states. It includes direct quotes from officials who are on the front lines of immigration enforcement in their states. Police Executive Research Forum is a police research and policy organization.

"Local Police Perspectives on State Immigration Policies," Police Executive Research Forum, July 2014. Reprinted by permission.

As you read, consider the following questions:

1. Why are states' approaches to immigration "fragmented"?
2. What connection can be made between certain states and the strictness of their immigration laws?
3. What is Houston's police chief trying to achieve by not having his officers enforce immigration laws?

B ecause immigration laws were being debated and approved in a number of states, PERF's round table discussion included federal law enforcement officials and police executives from Alabama, California, Georgia, South Carolina, Texas, and Virginia as well as Arizona. These participants provided critical insights into the legal developments taking place in each of their states.

It became clear from the discussion that immigration policy has become increasingly fragmented across the country, with states enacting individual laws that reflect their own political, demographic, and ideological landscapes. Some places, such as Alabama, Georgia, and South Carolina, have followed Arizona's lead in implementing strict immigration enforcement legislation. In other states, such as California and Texas, political and cultural shifts have caused officials to reject such tough measures.

Although states have chosen to address immigration issues in various ways, states as different as Arizona and California have something in common: They are taking it upon themselves to pass their own immigration policies, which has traditionally been the responsibility of the federal government.

States That Have Enacted Strict Immigration Laws

By mid-2011, states such as Alabama, Georgia, and South Carolina had passed tough immigration legislation patterned after SB 1070. Although the Supreme Court's 2012 decision in *Arizona v. United States* led federal courts to ultimately overturn many of these laws' provisions, courts have universally upheld immigration check requirements as valid and enforceable.

Alabama

In June 2011 Alabama enacted HB 56, a law that many considered stricter and more wide-reaching than Arizona SB 1070. Like Arizona's law, HB 56 requires police officers to make a reasonable attempt to establish a person's immigration status during a lawful stop, detention, or arrest if there is a reasonable suspicion that the individual is in the country illegally. HB 56 also includes a prohibition against using race, color, or national origin during enforcement.

In the wake of the U.S. Supreme Court's ruling on SB 1070, in August 2012 the U.S. Court of Appeals for the Eleventh Circuit upheld HB 56's status check requirement, but struck down the portions of the law that made it criminal for undocumented immigrants to seek work or fail to carry valid identification documents. The Circuit Court also upheld a provision that requires officers to make a reasonable e ort to determine citizenship within 48 hours if a driver does not have a valid driver's license in his or her possession.

Reaction to HB 56 has been mixed. Selma Police Chief William T. Riley III said that, although there was considerable public support for HB 56, concerns about racially biased policing and civil rights violations also prompted intense opposition to the law. Chief Riley said that hundreds of protesters organized a march from Montgomery to Selma to protest the law, echoing the civil rights demonstrations from the 1960s.

Georgia

In 2011, Georgia passed HB 87, which gave local police officers *the authority* to conduct immigration checks during lawful stops, arrests, or detentions if there is a reasonable suspicion that the person is in the country illegally. Unlike the provisions in Arizona and Alabama, immigration checks are optional under HB 87, meaning that officers have the discretion—but are not required—to conduct status checks in these situations.

Because the immigration check provision is optional in Georgia, its enforcement can vary greatly from jurisdiction to jurisdiction. "Different jurisdictions are all doing things differently," said Chief Kenneth DeSimone of the Sandy Springs, Georgia Police Department. In many places, agencies have simply chosen to not enforce immigration checks at all.

Chief DeSimone also discussed some of the misperceptions surrounding immigration in Georgia. "My community has a sizeable Hispanic community, but we've also had an influx of immigrants from the Middle East," said Chief DeSimone. "When we talk about immigration, we're not just talking about Hispanics. We're also talking about immigrants from the Middle East, Eastern Europe, and Asia."

South Carolina
South Carolina is another state that enacted strict immigration laws in the wake of Arizona SB 1070. In 2011, South Carolina passed SB 20, which contained an immigration status check requirement similar that in SB 1070. A July 2013 ruling in the U.S. Court of Appeals for the Fourth Circuit invalidated many of SB 20's provisions in accordance with the U.S. Supreme Court's 2012 ruling on the Arizona law, but let stand the requirement that officers conduct immigration checks during lawful stops, detentions, and arrests. As in other states, South Carolina's immigrant community has expressed fears that SB 20 will lead to racially biased policing, deportation, targeting of immigrants even if they are in the United States legally, and families being split apart.

Tony Fisher, the Executive Director of the Department of Public Safety in Spartanburg, South Carolina, worries that SB 20 creates many problems for local police officers. Federal immigration laws are extremely complex, and even immigration lawyers and federal officials who have spent years specializing in this field can find the laws daunting. It is not possible to adequately summarize federal immigration policy, laws and regulations in a brief training

What Taxpayers Need to Know When Cities Declare Themselves Sanctuaries

Cities across Southern California have named themselves immigrant-friendly "sanctuary cities" as they take a stand against President-elect Donald Trump's pledge to deport millions living in the country illegally.

But their actions are not without risks — political, legal and budgetary. So what should taxpayers know when their officials declare their cities as sanctuaries?

For La Puente, which last week declared itself a sanctuary city, it's a calculated risk, said City Manager David Carmany.

City officials have weighed the potential loss of federal funds. The city expects to receive about $2.3 million this year from Washington, D.C., coming through community development block grants and funds for services that include public safety, transportation and recreation.

The federal money adds to the city's roughly $12 million general fund. Nonetheless, "we think the principle of treating people decently is more important than some fear of losing federal money," Carmany said.

Cities have defined their sanctuary policies differently and it remains unclear which practices might trigger federal repercussions.

Carmany said the La Puente's sanctuary resolution doesn't change current practices concerning law enforcement or city services. The city contracts with the L.A. County Sheriff's Department for police services; Sheriff's officials have stated that the agency will not detain anyone solely on suspicion of being in the country illegally.

But Carmany said the La Puente City Council wanted to make a public statement "because our community has a lot of people who are very fearful right now." Carmany said post-election concerns have caused city officials to worry that immigrant residents won't report crimes, or will fear sending their children to school.

But California cities shouldn't be jeopardizing their federal funding, said John Berry, a Tea Party activist in Redlands who opposes sanctuary policies. Should cities defy the incoming administration and do lose out, they can't say they haven't been warned, he said.

"Whether it's a penny, a dollar or a million dollars, the point is that that's our money coming back from Washington," Berry said. "And it's going to be denied because the city made a choice to engage to protect illegal residents."

"What taxpayers need to know when cities declare themselves sanctuaries," by Leslie Berestein Rojas, Southern California Public Radio, January 17, 2017.

program for line officers. "Often, the local officers do not fully understand the law that they are supposed to be enforcing," said Director Fisher. "Police need to be careful that they are enforcing the law properly, in a way that is fair and that does not open us up to lawsuits."

Virginia

In 2007, nearly three years before Arizona SB 1070 went into effect, Prince William County, Virginia, passed a tough anti-immigration law that required police to inquire about the immigration status of any person that they stopped, detained, or arrested if there was probable cause to believe that the person was in the country illegally. In many ways a precursor to SB 1070, the controversial Prince William County law "helped spur similar efforts in Arizona and Alabama, spread panic among Latinos, and created emotional confrontations that tore at the fabric of [the] Northern Virginia county," according to a *Washington Post* article.

Amid the growing controversy, the Prince William County Board of Supervisors significantly amended the law one month after it took effect. The new version—which is much narrower than SB 1070 and its counterparts—requires police to conduct an immigration status check only when a person is arrested and in physical custody. The County also joined a federal program, known as 287(g), which established a formal partnership between local police and ICE.

To help smooth implementation and calm the growing fear and tension within the community, Prince William County Police Chief Charlie Deane implemented extensive training, community outreach, and evaluation efforts. He described his three-phase approach:

> First, we trained officers on the agency's core philosophy, which included protecting victims, focusing on those who commit crimes, and not allowing racial profiling. Second, we embarked on an extensive community outreach effort. My staff and I attended 200 to 300 community meetings to discuss what the

policy meant and how we would be enforcing it. Finally, we obtained funds to conduct an independent evaluation of how we implemented the law. We saw this as a way of holding ourselves and policymakers responsible; we wanted to make sure that we were having the intended impact and to assess the community's feelings about what the police were doing.

—Prince William County, VA Police Chief Charlie Deane

Many observers have praised Chief Deane's efforts, which were chronicled in the documentary "9500 Liberty," as a model approach for mitigating potentially harmful effects of strict immigration enforcement laws. Chief Deane's experiences are detailed further in later sections of this publication.

Outside of Prince William County, statewide efforts to implement immigration enforcement policies in Virginia have been mixed. In 2010, then-Attorney General Ken Cuccinelli issued an opinion stating that law enforcement officers in the State have the *option* of conducting an immigration status check during other lawful stops—not just arrests—if they have a "reasonable articulable suspicion" that the person came into the country illegally. In 2011, the Virginia House of Delegates proposed a set of sweeping immigration enforcement reforms similar to those in Arizona SB 1070. Although the legislation did not ultimately become law, opinion polls from 2012 showed that Virginia voters favored these types of strict measures. In 2013, Virginia passed a law banning illegal immigrants from obtaining concealed weapons permits.

A Moderate Approach

While Arizona and some Southeastern states have enacted increasingly strict immigration laws, some states, such as Texas and California, have grown more moderate. Cultural and political factors have led these states to shift away from strict enforcement policies.

California

When it comes to recent immigration laws, California sits on the opposite end of the spectrum from Arizona. In October 2013,

California Gov. Jerry Brown signed into law a set of sweeping bills that gave undocumented immigrants more rights than in anywhere else in the country. The state's recent pro-immigrant stance is in contrast to the 1990s, when California passed a controversial law that banned illegal immigrants from receiving health care, public education, and other services.[61] A court ultimately overturned that law, and over the past two decades strict immigration enforcement laws have fallen out of favor in the state. is this attributed partly to the emergence of California's large and increasingly powerful Hispanic community, and partly to the federal government's actions to control immigration along the California border. As the flow of immigration has moved toward the Arizona-Mexico border, which is now the country's primary entry point for undocumented immigrants from Mexico, the battle over immigration has shifted eastward as well.

At the center of California's 2013 reforms is the Transparency and Responsibility Using State Tools (Trust) Act, which provides that illegal immigrants who are placed under arrest would have to be charged with or convicted of a serious or violent felony to be subjected to a 48-hour hold and transfer to federal immigration authorities. Many police departments in California, including those in Los Angeles, Santa Clara, and San Francisco, had already implemented policies similar to those in the Trust Act. San Diego Police Chief William Lansdowne is one of the many California police executives who supported the Trust Act. "One of the most positive things about the Trust Act is that it targets serious offenders, but it is not so broad that it also targets people who have lived and worked in California for 20 years but then are picked up on some minor charge," said Chief Lansdowne. "The immigrant community was actually largely in favor of the Trust Act, because they too believe that people should be deported if they commit a serious crime."

Along with the Trust Act, the 2013 reforms also made it possible for illegal immigrants to obtain California driver's licenses. Los Angeles Police Chief Charlie Beck had long been a proponent of this policy, in part because it would lessen the burden of enforcing the state's strict vehicle impound laws, which allows officers to impound vehicles of unlicensed drivers for up to 30 days. Police chiefs in the state's major cities, including Chief Lansdowne and Chief Beck, had joined together to instruct their officers to stop enforcing the impound law. Chief Lansdowne recalled a story that highlighted the burden that the impound laws placed on drivers and officers:

> It was around 11:00 p.m. on Christmas Eve 2010, and while driving down a street I spotted a car that had been pulled over by one of my patrol officers. I pulled up behind the officer to check on the situation. I learned that the officer had planned to arrest the driver, a mother traveling with four small children, because she did not have a driver's license. The officer was also going to have the woman's car towed and report her to ICE. I instructed the officer to let the woman go. Our policy says that you cannot question someone about their immigration status for any traffic violation. If it happens, the officer will be reprimanded.
>
> *—San Diego, CA Police*
> *Chief William Lansdowne*

With illegal immigrants now able to obtain driver's licenses in California, Chief Lansdowne believes that his department will face fewer situations such as this.

Texas
In 2011, Texas Gov. Rick Perry made a considerable push to curb illegal immigration into Texas. He lobbied for legislation that mirrored Arizona SB 1070, including the creation of an "anti-sanctuary cities" law that would enable police officers to check the immigration status of any person suspected of not being a legal citizen.

The proposed bill did not pass, and no further attempts have been made at passing similar legislation. Enthusiasm for immigration enforcement measures appears to have waned in Texas; during the first half of 2013, the Texas legislature adopted 96 resolutions commending the contributions of immigrants and seeking federal action on immigration. This shift away from strict immigration policy has been attributed to efforts by both political parties to court the state's growing Hispanic vote.

Assistant Chief Daniel Perales of the Houston Police Department said that his department is committed to the principle that effective law enforcement depends upon good relationships between the Department and the community it serves, and that officers must rely upon the cooperation of all persons, including citizens and documented and undocumented immigrants, in their effort to maintain public order and combat crime. Therefore, he said, Houston police officers operate under a General Order, which was implemented in 1992, that prohibits officers from inquiring about immigration status unless a person has been arrested and placed in a city jail. Assistant Chief Perales said, "at the time of issuance of this General Order, the goal of this policy was to repair the deteriorating relationship between police and the Hispanic community."

> *"We're just trying to build cooperation in our communities. We don't really want people to be fearful of us because we're just trying to do our jobs to investigate any incidents and get cooperation from witnesses and victims."*

Local Law Enforcement Is Not Responsible for Immigration Enforcement

Andrew Ba Tran

In the following viewpoint, Andrew Ba Tran explores the definition of a sanctuary city, and focuses specifically on what implications this designation has in the state of Connecticut. It explains Connecticut's Trust Act, which gives local law enforcement officers the ability to ignore federal detainers issued against undocumented immigrants. It also explores the state of immigrant populations in Connecticut cities, as well as crime rates and potential federal repercussions for being sanctuary cities. Andrew Ba Tran is a data editor at the Connecticut Mirror.

"What It Means to Be A 'Sanctuary City' in Connecticut," CT Mirror, February 13, 2017. Reprinted by permission.

As you read, consider the following questions:

1. What is the misleading definition of sanctuary cities, as compared to the actual definition?
2. What is Connecticut's "Trust Act"?
3. Which two Connecticut cities have the largest immigrant populations? Why would they support the Trust Act?

Connecticut officials and protestors have come out against President Donald Trump's executive order to pull federal funding from so-called sanctuary cities.

But what are they, and what policies do they follow that federal immigration authorities object to?

What Are Sanctuary Cities?

The term "sanctuary city" is misleading, said Kari Hong, a Boston College law professor who specializes in immigration.

"It implies that [a state or municipality] gives amnesty to undocumented immigrants in defiance of the law, but it doesn't do that," she said. "It simply means they are not going to do the work of a federal officer in enforcing immigration law."

The federal government has to enforce the laws and not local police or agencies. Federal officials are responsible for their own agents, gathering their own information, and holding suspects in their own detention facilities. Phone calls and email messages to U.S. Immigration and Customs Enforcement were not returned.

Sanctuary in Connecticut

In 2013, Connecticut passed the "Trust Act" that allows state and local law enforcement agencies to ignore a federal "detainer" for an undocumented resident who hasn't committed a serious felony or been identified for other reasons, such as being in a database of gang members or suspected terrorists. A detainer is a request from immigration authorities to hold undocumented residents beyond their normal release date.

The federal government first began asking cities and states to work with them on deportation enforcement by running background checks on those they arrested and then detaining any undocumented suspects indefinitely until Immigration and Customs Enforcement officials (ICE) could determine whether they were deportable under President George W. Bush's Secure Communities Program, said Hong. This eventually evolved into President Barack Obama's Priority Enforcement Program.

Cities cooperated at first, but things changed. Federal officials told cities they would get rid of serious criminals like drug dealers, rapists, and murderers, but statistics showed that about 40 percent of those deported had no criminal record and 16 percent were deported for minor crimes, such as driving without a driver's license, Hong said.

States and cities sometimes were stuck detaining immigrants for years as cases were backlogged in immigration courts. Many jurisdictions were not reimbursed by the federal government, costing millions. Researchers also said immigrants were less likely to contact police officers if they had been a victim of a crime if they feared they or someone they knew would be asked about their immigration status.

It's not an issue that local agencies in Connecticut deal with often, said Monroe Police Chief John Salvatore, who is president of the Connecticut Police Chiefs Association.

It's not a necessity for local police to determine whether or not someone is undocumented, he said.

"We're just trying to build cooperation in our communities," said Salvatore. "We don't really want people to be fearful of us because we're just trying to do our jobs to investigate any incidents and get cooperation from witnesses and victims. We don't want them fearful of us."

Hartford and New Haven, which have a large immigrant populations, are among dozens of cities in Connecticut with police departments that have established policies of not asking the immigration status of those they arrest or those who contact police.

Colleges also may decline to cooperate with federal officials who ask for lists of noncitizen students. But if federal officials obtain an arrest or search warrant, then colleges must cooperate.

Immigrants in Connecticut

The percent of foreign-born residents in Connecticut grew from 8.5 percent in 1990 to 14 percent in 2015, according to figures from the U.S. Census. About 24 percent of the immigrants in Connecticut are undocumented, which ranks it 31st among the states in the percentage of immigrants who are undocumented, according to a study from Pew Research Center in 2014.

Crime in Sanctuary Cities

During his presidential campaign and since, Trump has characterized the policies followed in sanctuary policies as encouraging crime.

"I'm very much opposed to sanctuary cities. They breed crime. There's a lot of problems," Trump said during an interview with Bill O'Reilly of Fox News this week.

A recent study of 608 sanctuary counties found lower rates of crime there than in non-sanctuary counties.

Crime trends in Connecticut cities where officials have proclaimed sanctuary status show a consistent decline since the '90s.

Though there was a slight recent uptick in rates in some cities like Hartford and Manchester, the rates are still low relative to 20 years earlier.

The Legality

Can President Trump withhold federal funding from Connecticut and its cities for not cooperating with immigration enforcement?

There are Supreme Court precedents that prevent the federal government from commandeering local and state officials.

"He's making these threats with the executive order, but the Supreme Court have already said in a general manner that this won't be permitted," said Hong. "So it very much appears this is an attempt to coerce or bully or shame cities."

Two cities in Massachusetts, Lawrence and Chelsea, already have sued President Trump for his threat to cut federal funding. San Francisco filed a similar suit last week.

Enforcement of Trump's other executive order regarding immigration, which banned travel from seven Muslim-majority countries, has been blocked by the courts so far. The Trump administration is reportedly considering appealing to the U.S. Supreme Court or redrafting the executive order.

Since the terrorist attacks of Sept. 11, 2001, no one has been killed in the United States in a terrorist attack by anyone who emigrated from, or whose parents emigrated from, the seven countries targeted in the executive order: Syria, Iraq, Iran, Libya, Somalia, Sudan and Yemen.

Below are statistics for persons from those countries deported, and the proportion deported for criminal activity. (Libya's figures were not released by Homeland Security). Overall, they are an extremely small percentage of deportations from the U.S.

"*Scores of [sanctuary] cities...are standing resolute, with officials from over three dozen of them publicly reaffirming their commitment to 'basic human decency.'*"

Sanctuary Cities Allow Immigrants to Become a Contributing Part of the Community

Andrea Germanos

In the following viewpoint, Andrea Germanos explores the definition of sanctuary cities, which may be broader than many people know. Some cities may or may not officially declare themselves as sanctuary cities, but they may still function in the same way. The author cites statistics and research that contradict the claims made by opponents of sanctuary cities, such as higher crime rates. She also provides several examples of current sanctuary cities and why they have decided to provide refuge for immigrants. Andrea Germanos is a senior editor staff writer for Common Dreams.

As you read, consider the following questions:

1. What has research shown about sanctuary cities and crime rates?
2. What are some of the ways that US cities become sanctuary cities without actually defining themselves that way?
3. Why did some cities declare themselves sanctuary cities only after the 2017 election?

With Donald Trump's inauguration just over a month away, it will soon become clear whether he intends on using beginning days in the White House to try to follow through on his promise to end federal funding for sanctuary cities. Scores of such cities, however, are standing resolute, with officials from over three dozen of them publicly reaffirming their commitment to "basic human decency."

Sanctuary cities, sometimes called Fourth Amendment cities, as *The Atlantic*'s CityLab has described, offer some protection to undocumented immigrants because they "keep local policing and federal immigration enforcement separate by asking local police to decline 'detainers'—non-binding requests from ICE asking for extended detention of inmates they suspect are deportable."

In contrast to claims made by proponents of harsh immigrant crackdowns, research has shown that "designating a city as a sanctuary has no statistically significant effect on crime." In fact, it is harsh immigration policing that can negatively impact the whole community.

According to a new tally by Politico, out of a total of 47 sanctuary cities, "officials in at least 37 cities (listed below) have doubled down since Trump's election, reaffirming their current policies or practices in public statements, despite the threat of pushback from the incoming administration, and at least four cities have newly declared themselves sanctuary cities since Trump's win."

"There is no definitive list of U.S. sanctuary cities because of the term's flexible definition," the publication notes, and that itself may make it more problematic for Trump to ban the federal funds.

As Kica Matos, director of immigrant rights and racial justice at the Center for Community Change, explained to Fairness & Accuracy in Reporting last month, "sanctuary cities are understood as places that protect the undocumented immigrant and provide a haven for them and provide the opportunity for immigrants, irrespective of their status, to be welcomed, to be productive citizens in their respective communities, and to engage in the civic life of the cities."

> So if you look at some of the anti-immigrant organizations, Center for Immigrant Studies has a broader definition of sanctuary city, where they define sanctuary cities as any city that is friendly towards immigrants. So where I live, for example, New Haven, Connecticut, it's considered a sanctuary city under their definition, because the city implemented a program to offer city identification cards to any resident of the city, irrespective of their status. So if you go by that broader definition, there are hundreds of sanctuary cities in the United States, and many of them are already engaged in acts of defiance, publicly letting the federal government know that they will do absolutely everything they can to protect immigrants in their communities.

That broader definition seems to apply to Boulder, Colo., where city leaders are hoping to pass an ordinance before inauguration day to make it a sanctuary city—though whether or not the term 'sanctuary' actually ends up in the ordinance is unclear at this point.

Santa Ana, Calif., as Politico writes, is like the Vermont cities of Burlington, Montpelier, and Winooski in that it declared itself a sanctuary city post-election.

"The day after Donald Trump got elected, our kids were falling apart emotionally. They thought their parents would be deported," the Los Angeles Times quotes said Sal Tinajero, a Santa Ana City Council member and local high school teacher, as saying.

"The reason you're seeing this push now is that us leaders ... want to tell them they are going to be protected. If they are going to come for them, they have to come through us first," Tinajero said.

Somerville, Mass., meanwhile, is among the cities on Politico's tally that have reaffirmed their commitments. In an open letter published last month, Somerville Mayor Joseph A. Curtatone wrote, "We will not turn our back on our neighbors. Our diversity is our strength. Since we became a sanctuary city [in 1987], our crime rate has dropped more than 50%."

So "for anyone who claims that cracking down on sanctuary cities has something to do with high crime or a stagnant economy, Somerville stands as a flashing, neon billboard for how wrong that thinking is," he continued.

"If cities have to make a stand for basic human decency, then we're going to make that stand. We saw a presidential campaign based on fear and a desire to ostracize anyone who could be categorized as different. That may have swung an election, but it provides us with no roadmap forward. Tearing communities apart only serves to tear them down. We're going to keep bringing people together, making sure we remain a sanctuary for all. We are one community. We've got values that work. We know what makes America great," Curtatone concludes.

Also among Trump's anti-immigrant promises is a pledge to deport "more than two million criminal illegal immigrants from the country"—which he clarified to mean people who haven't actually been convicted of a crime.

> *"Law enforcement agencies across the country have found that the most effective ways to encourage crime reporting by immigrants and all residents are to engage in tried and true initiatives ... not by suspending cooperation with federal immigration enforcement efforts."*

Sanctuary Cities Are Protecting Criminals
Dan Cadman and Jessica Vaughan

In the following excerpted viewpoint Dan Cadman and Jessica Vaughan argue that sanctuary cities are flagrantly disregarding federal law and obstructing the efforts of federal immigration officials. They discuss the different options available to President Trump for dealing with sanctuary cities, especially those who have openly stated that they will not cooperate with his executive order, and cite several of the laws that these cities are violating. They also state the reasons and justifications provided by sanctuary cities for disregarding federal laws, and refute these arguments by citing studies to the contrary. Dan Cadman is a retired INS/ICE official and a current Fellow at the Center for Immigration Studies. Jessica Vaughan is Director of Policy Studies for the Center for Immigration Studies.

"Tackling Sanctuaries," by Dan Cadman and Jessica Vaughan, Center for Immigration Studies, December 13, 2016. Reprinted by permission.

As you read, consider the following questions:

1. How do sanctuary cities protect criminals?
2. How do some college campuses become classified as sanctuaries? What specifically do they do?
3. What alternatives do law enforcement officials have for encouraging crime reporting from immigrants, besides declaring themselves to be sanctuary cities?

Introduction and Background

The Center for Immigration Studies has tracked the movement, repeatedly spoken out against it,[1] and watched as it has grown under the policies of the Obama White House, whose aims have more closely mirrored those of open borders advocates than those of an administration constitutionally charged with faithfully executing the laws of the United States.[2] There are now more than 300 state and local governments with laws, rules, or policies that impede federal efforts to enforce immigration laws.[3] In the past several years, a "sanctuary" movement has arisen in various states and political subdivisions around the country. This movement intends to, and does in fact, obstruct the efforts of federal officers to enforce immigration laws, substituting instead the views of the state or local jurisdiction over how or whether immigration laws will be enforced within its boundaries.

Donald Trump began his dark horse presidential candidacy by campaigning to restore respect for America's borders and its immigration laws. Included in his platform was the message that sanctuaries which flouted those laws would not be tolerated. In his immigration policy speech in Phoenix in August, Trump said:

> Block funding for sanctuary cities ... no more funding. We will end the sanctuary cities that have resulted in so many needless deaths. Cities that refuse to cooperate with federal authorities will not receive taxpayer dollars, and we will work with Congress to pass legislation to protect those jurisdictions that do assist federal authorities.

Mr. Trump's platform resonated with voters and he is now president-elect.

Reacting to Trump's election, a number of sanctuary cities have declared that they will not retreat from their existing policies. The statements from Mayors Rahm Emanuel of Chicago and Bill DeBlasio of New York, as well as a number of others, have had a particular "throw down the gauntlet" tone to them.[4] Several police chiefs have taken a similar approach,[5] and one governor has threatened to sue the federal government if it withholds funds from sanctuaries.[6]

In addition, the students and faculty at a number of colleges and universities nationwide have demanded that administrators declare their campuses to be sanctuaries.[7] A publicly supported university in Oregon has done this,[8] as have the private Wesleyan and Columbia Universities. Meanwhile these schools collect millions of dollars in federal research funds and are the happy beneficiaries of additional millions from students using federal Pell grants and federally-subsidized student loans to pay for their tuition.[9]

But even many of those institutions which do not declare themselves sanctuaries already openly accept illegal alien students, in flagrant disregard of the immigration laws, and offer them in-state tuition rates. Ironically, this includes the University of California system, whose president is Janet Napolitano, former secretary of the Department of Homeland Security (DHS) under the Obama administration. The UC system goes so far as to provide an online Undocumented Student Resources guide, declaring that "Undocumented students of all ethnicities and nationalities can find a safe environment and supportive community at the University of California...UC campuses offer a range of support services—from academic and personal counseling, to financial aid and legal advising..."[10]

The purpose of this paper is to consider the means available to the Trump administration to confront and dissuade sanctuaries and diminish their ability to impede enforcement of federal immigration laws.

What is a "Sanctuary"?

Different people and groups may have different definitions of a sanctuary, and there is a spectrum of such policies across the nation. For our purposes, a sanctuary is a jurisdiction that has a law, ordinance, policy, practice, or rule that deliberately obstructs immigration enforcement, restricts interaction with federal immigration agencies, or shields illegal aliens from detection. In addition, federal law includes two key provisions that forbid certain practices: one that forbids policies restricting communication and information sharing (8 U.S.C. Section 1373) and one that forbids harboring illegal aliens or shielding them from detection (8 U.S.C. Section 1324).

Information exchanges
8 U.S.C. 1373 states:

> a Federal, State, or local government entity or official may not prohibit, or in any way restrict, any government entity or official from sending to, or receiving from, [federal immigration authorities] information regarding the citizenship or immigration status, lawful or unlawful, of any individual.

A recent report from the Department of Justice's Office of Inspector General (DOJ OIG)11, requested by Rep. John Culberson (R-Texas), who chairs the appropriations committee in charge of the DOJ budget, determined that sanctuary policies which prohibit local officers from communicating or exchanging information with ICE are "inconsistent" with federal law. Sanctuary jurisdictions do this by ignoring immigration detainers, which are filed by Immigration and Customs Enforcement (ICE) agents to signal their intent to take custody of aliens for purposes of removal, once state or local justice system proceedings are concluded. Some jurisdictions go further by prohibiting communication to advise or even acknowledge to ICE agents that the alien has been arrested. They also sometimes prevent ICE agents from access to the alien to conduct interviews.

The OIG report investigated the policies of 10 jurisdictions and found that they did indeed limit cooperation with ICE in an improper way:

> [E]ach of the 10 jurisdictions had laws or policies directly related to how those jurisdictions could respond to ICE detainers, and each limited in some way the authority of the jurisdiction to take action with regard to ICE detainers...We also found that the laws and policies in several of the 10 jurisdictions go beyond regulating responses to ICE detainers and also address, in some way, the sharing of information with federal immigration authorities.

Harboring Aliens in Violation of Law
8 U.S.C. 1324 states:

> Any person who...knowing or in reckless disregard of the fact that an alien has come to, entered, or remains in the United States in violation of law, conceals, harbors, or shields from detection, or attempts to conceal, harbor, or shield from detection, such alien in any place, ...; encourages or induces an alien to come to, enter, or reside in the United States, knowing or in reckless disregard of the fact that such coming to, entry, or residence is or will be in violation of law; or engages in any conspiracy to commit any of the preceding acts, or aids or abets the commission of any of the preceding acts, shall be....fined under title 18, imprisoned not more than 5 years, or both...[12]

Much of the sanctuary movement seems to be centered on shielding from federal action deportable aliens who have been arrested and charged with various crimes. But other jurisdictions have more expansive policies aimed at shielding some or all illegal aliens, including the so-called Dreamers and their families, from enforcement action.

What are the Arguments Made by Sanctuary Advocates?

The arguments have several distinct but interrelated themes:

- Police cooperation with immigration agents erodes trust between immigrants and authorities, and causes immigrants to refrain from reporting crimes;
- We don't want to act as immigration agents;
- We don't get reimbursed for incarceration costs;
- Cooperation is voluntary;
- Detainers must be accompanied by warrants;
- States are sovereign entities that have the right to make their own decisions on immigration.

In our view, when examined critically none of these arguments holds water, except for the one having to do with warrants, and that argument holds only to a certain degree, which we will discuss further below.

Police cooperation compromises community trust and safety
One of the most common reasons offered for non-cooperation policies is that they are needed so that immigrants will have no fear of being turned over for deportation when they report crimes. This frequently-heard claim has never been substantiated, and in fact has been refuted by a number of reputable studies. Not a shred of evidence of a "chilling effect" on immigrant crime reporting when local police cooperate with ICE exists in federal or local government or police data or independent academic research.

It is important to remember that crime reporting can be a problem in any place, and is not confined to any one segment of the population. In fact, most crimes are not reported, regardless of the victim's immigration status or ethnicity. According to the Bureau of Justice Statistics (BJS), in 2015, only 47 percent of violent victimizations, 55 percent of serious violent victimizations, were reported to police. In 2015, the percentage of property victimizations reported to police was just 35 percent.[13] These rates have been unaffected, either by changes in the level of interaction between local and federal enforcement from 2009-2012 (which coincides with the implementation of the Secure Communities biometric matching program) or by the spread of sanctuary policies since 2014.

Data from BJS show no meaningful differences among ethnic groups in crime reporting. Overall, Hispanics are slightly more likely to report crimes than other groups. Hispanic females, especially, are slightly more likely than white females and more likely than Hispanic and non-Hispanic males to report violent crimes.[14] This is consistent with academic surveys finding Hispanic females to be more trusting of police than other groups.[15]

A multitude of other studies refute the notion that local-federal cooperation in immigration enforcement causes immigrants to refrain from reporting crimes:

- A major study completed in 2009 by researchers from the University of Virginia and the Police Executive Research Forum (PERF) found no decline in crime reporting by Hispanics after the implementation of a local police program to screen offenders for immigration status and to refer illegal aliens to ICE for removal. This examination of Prince William County, Virginia's 287(g) program is the most comprehensive study to refute the "chilling effect" theory. The study also found that the county's tough immigration policies likely resulted in a decline in certain violent crimes.[16]
- The most reputable academic survey of immigrants and crime reporting found that by far the most commonly mentioned reason for not reporting a crime was a language barrier (47 percent), followed by cultural differences (22 percent), and a lack of understanding of the U.S. criminal justice system (15 percent) — not fear of being turned over to immigration authorities.[17]
- The academic literature reveals varying attitudes and degrees of trust toward police within and among immigrant

communities. Some studies have found that Central Americans may be less trusting than other groups, while others maintain that the most important factor is socio-economic status and feelings of empowerment within a community, rather than the presence or level of immigration enforcement.[18]

- A 2009 study of calls for service in Collier County, Fla., found that the implementation of the 287(g) partnership program with ICE enabling local sheriff's deputies to enforce immigration laws, resulting in significantly more removals of criminal aliens, did not affect patterns of crime reporting in immigrant communities.[19]
- Data from the Boston, Mass., Police Department, one of two initial pilot sites for ICE's Secure Communities program, show that in the years after the implementation of this program, which ethnic and civil liberties advocates alleged would suppress crime reporting, showed that calls for service decreased proportionately with crime rates. The precincts with larger immigrant populations had less of a decline in reporting than precincts with fewer immigrants.[20]
- Similarly, several years of data from the Los Angeles Police Department covering the time period of the implementation of Secure Communities and other ICE initiatives that increased arrests of aliens show that the precincts with the highest percentage foreign-born populations do not have lower crime reporting rates than precincts that are majority black, or that have a smaller foreign-born population, or that have an immigrant population that is more white than Hispanic. The crime reporting rate in Los Angeles is most affected by the amount of crime, not by race, ethnicity, or size of the foreign-born population.[21]
- Recent studies based on polling of immigrants about whether they might or might not report crimes in the future based on hypothetical local policies for police interaction with ICE, such as one recent study entitled "Insecure Communities", by

Nik Theodore of the University of Illinois, Chicago, should be considered with great caution, since they measure emotions and predict possible behavior, rather than record and analyze actual behavior of immigrants.[22] Moreover, the Theodore study is particularly flawed because it did not compare crime reporting rates of Latinos with other ethnic groups.

For these reasons, law enforcement agencies across the country have found that the most effective ways to encourage crime reporting by immigrants and all residents are to engage in tried and true initiatives such as community outreach, hiring personnel who speak the languages of the community, establishing anonymous tip lines, and setting up community sub-stations with non-uniform personnel to take inquiries and reports – not by suspending cooperation with federal immigration enforcement efforts. Proposals to increase ICE-local cooperation, such as the Davis-Oliver Act, which was passed by the House Judiciary Committee in 2015, enjoy strong support among law enforcement leaders across the country. These leaders — sheriffs, police, and state agency commanders — routinely and repeatedly express concern over crime problems associated with illegal immigration and routinely and repeatedly express their willingness to assist ICE, and that it is their duty to assist ICE.[23] The National Sheriffs Association and numerous individual sheriffs and police chiefs have endorsed the Davis-Oliver Act.

Instead of pushing sanctuary policies, advocates for immigrants in the community should be stressing that victims and witnesses are never targets for immigration enforcement (unless they, too, are criminals). If immigrant advocates would help disseminate this message, instead of spreading the myth that immigrants have something to fear from interaction with local police, then everyone in the community would be safer. It is important to remember that much of the crime inflicted on aliens comes from other aliens— for instance, coyotes, drug dealers, gangbangers and other career criminals—who prey on their own communities. When this is the case, alien victims and witnesses, significantly including aliens illegally in the United States, have every reason to want them plucked out of their midst by local law enforcement and removed by ICE.

What is more, aliens tend to be very familiar with the workings of immigration law, much more so than the average citizen, because it is in their interest to do so. As such, while they may not be able to cite specific visa categories, they are quite likely to know that immigration law and policy actually contain provisions to protect victims and witnesses from removal actions so that they can provide key information to police and prosecutors. If police officers want to be able to help immigrants who are victimized to take advantage of these programs, they need to have a good working relationship with ICE – and they also need to be allowed to inquire about immigration status so that they can offer this protection.

Lastly, we should point out that while state and local governments can't point to any credible studies to support their argument that cooperation with ICE diminishes trust levels in ethnic and alien communities, there is plenty of empirical, and powerful anecdotal, evidence which shows the damage done to communities when alien offenders are inappropriately released back to the street, whether by state and local police or by ICE, rather than being detained and removed from the United States for their offenses.[24] There have been so many victims of criminal behavior by illegal aliens that surviving family members of those killed have banded together to draw attention to their plight, and to the danger posed by sanctuary policies.[25] The families of these victims have been steadfastly ignored by law enforcement organizations and governments engaged in sanctuary policies, and they were ignored by the Democratic party during the presidential campaign. (Even before that, one Democratic representative went so far as to refer to the murder of a young woman by a multiply deported illegal alien felon as "a little thing".[26]) But the families of the victims were not ignored by presidential candidate Trump; he embraced them publicly, and they appeared frequently with him on the campaign trail as he promised to address the problem of sanctuaries if elected.

[…]

End Notes

1 See, for instance, Mark Krikorian, "No Sanctuary for Sanctuary Cities", Center for Immigration Studies (CIS) blog, Feb. 25, 2009; http://cis.org/krikorian/no-sanctuary-sanctuary-cities and W.D. Reasoner, "Which Way, New York?" CIS blog, Oct. 2011. http://cis.org/nyc-local-interference

2 Article II, Section 3 of the United States Constitution requires that "[The President] shall take Care that the Laws be faithfully executed…." See, e.g.,"The Heritage Guide to the Constitution" http://www.heritage.org/constitution/articles/2/essays/98/take-care-clause.

3 For an interactive map of existing sanctuary locations, see Bryan Griffith and Jessica Vaughan, "Map: Sanctuary Cities, Counties, and States: Sanctuary Cities Continue to Obstruct Enforcement, Threaten Public Safety" CIS backgrounder, orig. Jan. 2016, updated Aug. 31, 2016. http://cis.org/Sanctuary-Cities-Map

4 Associated Press, "Mayor Rahm Emanuel says Chicago will remain sanctuary city for immigrants" The Herald News, Nov. 14, 2016 http://www.theherald-news.com/2016/11/14/mayor-rahm-emanuel-says-chicago… ; David Goodman, " 'The Ball's in His Court,' Mayor de Blasio Says After Meeting With Trump", New York Times, Nov. 16, 2016 http://www.nytimes.com/2016/11/17/nyregion/donald-trump-mayor-bill-de-bl… ; Neil W. McCabe, "Mayor Trolls President-elect Trump: Take Our Federal Funds, We Will Stay a Sanctuary City Forever", Breitbart.com, Nov. 21, 2016. http://www.breitbart.com/big-government/2016/11/21/mayor-trolls-presiden… take-our-federal-funds-we-will-stay-a-sanctuary-city-forever/

5 See, for example, the statements made by the Los Angeles Police Department Chief: "Chief Beck: LAPD Will Not Aid Trump Deportation Efforts", Police Magazine, Nov. 15, 2016. http://www.policemag.com/channel/pa trol/news/2016/11/15/chief-beck-lapd-will-not-aid-trump-deportation-efforts.aspx

6 Mark Davis, "Malloy says he'll sue if Trump attempts to punish 'Sanctuary City' New Haven", News8 WTNH online, Nov. 22, 2016. http://wtnh.com/2016/11/22/malloy-says-hell-sue-if-trump-attempts-to-pun…

7 Edmund Kozak, "Students Rage for 'Sanctuary' Campuses: Fearful of Trump, college agitators demand colleges become safe spaces for illegal aliens" Lifezette online magazine, updated Nov. 17, 2016. http://www.lifezette.com/polizette/students-rage-sanctuary-campuses/ and John Binder, "Vanderbilt Students Demand 'Sanctuary Campus'", Breitbart.com, Nov. 28, 2016. http://www.breitbart.com/texas/2016/11/28/vanderbilt-students-demand-san…

8 "President Wim Wiewel declares PSU a sanctuary university", press announcement, Portland State University website, Nov. 18, 2016. http://www.pdx.edu/news/president-wim-wiewel-declares-psu-sanctuary-univ.

9 Blake Neff, "Columbia University Declares Itself a Sanctuary Campus for Illegal Immigrants", The Daily Caller, Nov. 21, 2016. http://dailycaller.com/2016/11/21/columbia-university-declares-itself-a-…

10 "Undocumented Student Resources", University of California website, accessed on December 2, 2016. http://undoc.universityofcalifornia.edu/

11 Memorandum from Michael E. Horowitz, Inspector General, "Department of Justice Referral of Allegations of Potential Violations of 8 USC 1373 by Grant Recipients," May 31, 2016, https://oig.justice.gov/reports/2016/1607.pdf.

12 With regard to the potential penalty, note, though, that the statute says, "in the case of a violation...resulting in the death of any person, be punished by death or imprisoned for any term of years or for life, fined under title 18, or both." An extreme reading of the statute might lead one to conclude that the actions of the San Francisco sheriff in releasing a multiply-deported alien felon which in turn led him to murder of Kate Steinle (discussed later in the body of this report) would subject him not only to prosecution but punishment under this enhancement of the available penalties.

13 Jennifer Truman, Ph.D., Lynn Langton, Ph.D., and Michael Planty, Ph.D., Bureau of Justice Statistics, "Crime Victimization 2012," http://www.bjs.gov/content/pub/pdf/cv12.pdf.

14 See additional data from the National Crime Victimization Survey here: http://www.bjs.gov/content/pub/pdf/cvus0805.pdf.

15 Lynn Langton, Marcus Berzofsky, Christopher Krebs, and Hope Smiley-McDonald, Bureau of Justice Statistics report, "Victimizations Not Reported to the Police, 2006-2010," http://www.bjs.gov/content/pub/ pdf/vnrp0610.pdf.

16 Evaluation Study of Prince William County's Illegal Immigration Enforcement Policy: FINAL REPORT 2010, http://www.pwcgov.org/government/dept/police/Documents/13185.pdf.

17 Robert C. Davis, Edna Erez and Nancy Avitabile, "Access to Justice for Immigrants Who are Victimized. The Perspectives of Police and Prosecutors" Criminal Justice Policy Review, 12(3): 183-196, 2001.

18 Menjivar, Cecilia and Cynthia L. Bejarano, "Latino Immigrants' Perceptions of Crime and Police Authorities in the United States: A Case Study from the Phoenix Metropolitan Area," Ethnic and Racial Studies 27(1): 120-148, 2004.

19 Commander Michael Williams, Collier County (Fla.) Sheriff's Office, as reported here: http://cis.org/files/articles/2009/leaps/index.htm.

20 Boston Police Department report on calls for service by precinct provided by Jessica Vaughan.

21 Los Angeles Police Department annual Statistical Digest, available at www.lapdonline.org.

22 Nik Theodore, "Insecure Communities: Latino Perceptions of Police Involvement in Immigration Enforcement", College of Urban Planning & Public Affairs, University of Illinois at Chicago, May 1, 2013. https://greatcities.uic.edu/2013/05/01/insecure-communities-latino-perce...

23 See for example, the remarks of sheriffs at these events by the Center for Immigration Studies: http://cis.org/Videos/Sanctuary-Cities-Panel, http://cis.org/Videos/Panel-Crime-Challenges, and http://cis.org/vaughan/sheriffs-skeptical-chilling-effect-secure-communi...

24 Jessica Vaughan, "The Non-Departed: 925,000 Aliens Ordered Removed Are Still Here" CIS backgrounder, June 30, 2016. http://cis.org/vaughan/non-departed-925000-aliens-ordered-removed-are-st...

25 See http://www.theremembranceproject.org/.

26 Mark Krikorian, "Kate Steinle Day", CIS blog, July 1, 2016, http://cis.org/krikorian/kate-steinle-day

> *"Harboring or shielding from detection any alien who 'remains in the United States in violation of law' is itself a violation of federal law."*

The Priority for Protection Should Be US Citizens, Not Immigrants

Joseph Klein

In the following viewpoint, Joseph Klein argues that sanctuary cities are harboring dangerous criminals at the expense of the safety of their own citizens. He cites several cases where undocumented or illegal immigrants are committing crimes, but despite their criminal records, are still being harbored and protected by sanctuary cities. The author contends that shielding these criminals is not only a violation of federal law, but also jeopardizes innocent people, and any law enforcement officers in these cities who protect criminals should themselves be fully prosecuted if one of these immigrants commits a crime. Joseph Klein is a lawyer and author.

"Sanctuary Cities Choose Criminals Over Citizens," by Joseph Klein, Frontpagemag.com, March 29, 2017. Reprinted by permission.

As you read, consider the following questions:

1. According to Jeff Sessions, how are cities harming their citizens by becoming sanctuary cities?
2. How is Chicago's mayor linking the city's future to organized crime?
3. Do illegal immigrants commit more crimes than American citizens, according to this article?

Attorney General Jeff Sessions warned on Monday that sanctuary jurisdictions risked losing federal grants if they persisted in obstructing the enforcement of federal immigration laws. Billions of dollars in federal law enforcement funding are at stake. "I urge the nation's states and cities to carefully consider the harm they are doing to their citizens by refusing to enforce our immigration laws," Attorney General Sessions said. "Countless Americans would be alive today and countless loved ones would not be grieving today if these policies of sanctuary cities were ended."

Instead of heeding the Attorney General's sound advice and taking care of their own citizens, city officials around the country are planning to sabotage federal law enforcement of the nation's immigration laws.

"We are going to become this administration's worst nightmare," said New York City Council Speaker Melissa Mark-Viverito. On the same day that Attorney General Sessions issued his warning, she hosted a meeting with like-minded officials from other sanctuary cities, including San Francisco, Seattle, Denver, Chicago, and Philadelphia, who prioritize the welfare of illegal immigrants over their own citizens. Ms. Mark-Viverito and her comrades threatened to block access by federal immigration authorities to city property and to city records that could help with the enforcement of the nation's immigration laws. They are acting in the spirit of Alabama's late Governor George Wallace, who stood in the schoolhouse door to defy federal enforcement of desegregation.

"The Trump Administration is pushing an unrealistic and mean spirited executive order," tweeted New York City Mayor Bill de Blasio. Spare us the tears, Mr. Mayor. We are not talking about innocent children caught up in vindictive mass deportation sweeps. Rather, President Trump's so-called "mean-spirited executive order" is intended to rid this country of fiends like Estivan Rafael Marques Velasquez, a gang member from El Salvador with a criminal record, who was released from Rikers Island this year onto the streets of New York before U.S. officers from the Immigration and Customs Enforcement (ICE) unit could pick him up for deportation proceedings. And there is Luis Alejandro Villegas, 31, who was released from local custody on Dec. 31, 2016, despite a detainer request from ICE. Villegas had previously been removed from the United States and has a prior conviction for forcible theft armed with a deadly weapon.

"Villegas is a criminal alien who was released back into our New York communities, posing an increased and unnecessary risk to those who live in this great city," said Thomas R. Decker, field office director for ICE's Enforcement and Removal Operations in New York.

Fortunately, ICE agents were able to catch up with both Velasquez and Villegas on their own and place them into federal custody. If de Blasio has his way, we may not be so lucky next time. In the New York City suburb of Hempstead, two women and a 2-year old girl ran out of luck. A MS-13 street gang member, who had been deported back to El Salvador from the U.S. four times and had a number of prior arrests, stabbed the women and sexually assaulted the little girl.

Hempstead is in Nassau County, which is a sanctuary jurisdiction. Hempstead's Mayor Wayne J. Hall, Sr. said last February, "President Trump's recent executive orders go against the moral fiber with which our great nation was built, and I wholeheartedly support New York City Mayor Bill DeBlasio and countless other Mayors throughout the United States in denouncing these acts. I, Mayor DeBlasio and leaders from many other communities throughout the country will work together to oppose these executive orders and protect the rights of all people." Good going, Mayor Hall. Now you can explain your opposition to rounding up and deporting illegal aliens with prior criminal records to the illegal aliens' victims in your town, whom you should have been more worried about.

Chicago's Mayor Rahm Emanuel, who is presiding over a city beset by rampant crime, reiterated his pledge that Chicago will "continue to welcome" immigrants. "Chicago was built on the back of immigrants and our future is hitched to the wagon of immigrants who come to the city," he added. Do these include the 45 out of 48 illegal immigrants picked up in a raid last month in the Chicago area who had previously been convicted of crimes, including criminal sexual assault? Twenty of the illegal aliens had returned to the country after have been already deported. In refusing to cooperate with federal immigration enforcement officials, Mayor Emanuel is hitching Chicago's future in part to criminal illegal aliens who remain free to prey on Chicago's citizens.

Challenging the Trump administration's intention to put an end to sanctuary cities, Los Angeles Mayor Eric Garcetti said Monday that his city's policies are "designed to keep our residents safe." Tell that to the surviving family and friends of the Californian woman killed in a car crash caused by a drunk illegal alien with a long rap sheet,who had been deported previously. Perhaps Mayor Garcetti would do well to listen to the victim's fiancé, who blamed politicians like himself for the "criminal illegal immigrants that are being harbored here." Then again, Garcetti, Emanuel, de Blasio and the rest of the sanctuary city crowd are intent on placing their own pro-illegal alien progressive agenda above the safety and welfare of the people they are supposed to serve and protect.

In Travis County, Texas, Sheriff Sally Hernandez, known as "Sanctuary Sally," has adopted sanctuary policies for the county in defiance of both federal and Texas state law enforcement. "We can't have state and elected officials in the state like Sanctuary Sally [Hernandez] down here in Travis County turn a blind eye to releasing illegals that have felony convictions and then wonder what's going to happen when they get back into general population," said Texas District 7 Senator Paul Bettencourt. But it may be too late. According to a report issued by ICE on March 20, identifying those sanctuary jurisdictions which released criminal aliens under an immigration detainer, Sanctuary Sally's county scored the number 1 position. It's only a matter of time when a released illegal immigrant with felony convictions commits another crime.

Illegal immigrants in the United States make up approximately 3.5% of the nation's entire population. According to data compiled from the U.S. Sentencing Commission for fiscal year 2015, illegal immigrants were responsible for 30.2 percent of convictions for kidnapping/hostage taking, 17.8 percent of convictions for drug trafficking, 11.6 percent of convictions for fraud, 10.4 percent of convictions for money laundering, 6.1 percent of convictions for assault, and 5.5 percent of convictions for murder. So much for the myth spread by the pro-illegal immigrant crowd that illegal immigrants commit serious crimes at a much lower rate than U.S.-born citizens.

Harboring or shielding from detection any alien who "remains in the United States in violation of law" is itself a violation of federal law. It also has real life consequences for the victims of the crimes committed by illegal aliens who are being shielded in sanctuary jurisdictions. Local and state officials who willfully help illegal immigrants evade detention for possible deportation should be prosecuted to the fullest extent of the law.

Periodical and Internet Sources Bibliography

The following articles have been selected to supplement the diverse views presented in this chapter.

Darla Cameron, "How sanctuary cities work, and how Trump's blocked executive order could have affected them." Washington Post, November 7, 2017. https://www.washingtonpost.com/ graphics/national/sanctuary-cities/

Lauren Carasik, "Whom Do Sanctuary Cities Protect?" Boston Review, March 9, 2017. http://bostonreview.net/law-justice/ lauren-carasik-whom-do-sanctuary-cities-protect

Mary Fan, "How Sanctuary Cities Can Protect Dreamers." Fortune, September 7, 2017. http://fortune.com/2017/09/07/daca-program-sanctuary-cities-donald-trump-dreamers/

Matt Ford, "Federal Court Blocks Trump's Crackdown on Sanctuary Cities." The Atlantic, September 15, 2017. https://www.theatlantic.com/politics/archive/2017/09/federal-court-blocks-trump-crackdown-on-sanctuary-cities/540072/

Bryan Griffith and Jessica Vaughan," Maps: Sanctuary Cities, Counties, and States." Center for Immigration Studies, November 16, 2017. https://cis.org/Map-Sanctuary-Cities-Counties-and-States

Alex Kotlowitz, "The Limits of Sanctuary Cities." The New Yorker, November 23, 2016. https://www.newyorker.com/news/news-desk/the-limits-of-sanctuary-cities

Janell Ross, "6 big things to know about sanctuary cities." Washington Post, July 8, 2015. https://www.washingtonpost.com/news/the-fix/wp/2015/07/08/4-big-things-to-know-about-sanctuary-cities-and-illegal-immigration/?utm_term=.86ec5e2ddb5f

Amanda Sakuma, "No Safe Place." MSNBC Specials. Accessed January 4, 2018. http://www.msnbc.com/specials/migrant-crisis/ sanctuary-cities

Jonathan S. Tobin, "A Liberal Judge Rediscovers the Tenth Amendment — So Should Conservatives." National Review, November 22, 2017. http://www.nationalreview.com/ article/453994/sanctuary-cities-states-rights-honot-tenth-amendment

OPPOSING
VIEWPOINTS®
SERIES

CHAPTER 2

Are Crime Rates Higher in Sanctuary Cities?

Chapter Preface

O ne of the arguments most frequently used against sanctuary cities is that they create communities that are at a greater risk for serious crime. The debate over crime rates in sanctuary cities is a heated one, with some claiming that these cities are experiencing higher crime rates, and others claiming that regardless of crime rates, the undocumented immigrants are not the ones who are perpetrating these crimes.

One of the events most often used to illustrate the crime risk posed by illegal or undocumented immigrants took place in San Francisco in July of 2015. Kate Steinle, a 32-year-old woman, was taking an evening stroll along a pier in the city's Embarcadero area. Suddenly she was struck in the back by a bullet, and despite efforts to give her CPR, she died at the hospital just hours later. The man charged with shooting her was Jose Ines Garcia Zarate of Mexico, who had seven felony convictions and had been deported back to Mexico five times. He had recently spent several months in jail for a different crime, but was released. Immigration officials did not take him into custody or deport him. San Francisco's status as a sanctuary city was blamed for the crime, even though Zarate was acquitted of murder after a trial and convicted only of felony firearm possession. He claimed that the bullet accidentally ricocheted off the ground and hit Steinle.

Many American citizens and lawmakers have used Steinle's death as an example of what happens when sanctuary cities protect undocumented or illegal immigrants. However, there are many other cases where immigrants living in sanctuary cities, with no fear of deportation, have helped to prevent crimes or defuse situations where crime might take place. Both sides have come forward with statistics on crime that supposedly prove their side of the issue, and the topic is still hotly debated both by communities and federal and state lawmakers.

> *"If the law is unjust, you have to disobey it. To me you're not a church if you say no. I mean, what does it mean to say that I'm Christian only up to my nation's boundary?"*

Faith Communities and Campuses Should Be Refuges for Immigrants

Rebekah Barber

In the following viewpoint, Rebekah Barber contends that there is a resurgence of college campuses and religious institutions offering refuge and protection to immigrants. The idea of providing sanctuary goes back thousands of years, and some of the first institutions to offer a place of safety were churches and universities. With today's sanctuary cities under attack by both federal and state governments and authorities, faith communities feel that it is part of their religious convictions to offer refuge, and college campuses feel that they should protect their undocumented students. Barber is a researcher and writer at Institute for Southern Studies.

As you read, consider the following questions:

1. Why are colleges and churches becoming refuges for immigrants?
2. What is meant by "modern underground railroads"?
3. How are cities responding to President Trump's executive order banning sanctuary cities?

D ating back thousands of years, the concept of sanctuary stems from the custom of offering hospitality to the stranger. In ancient Greek cities, slaves and thieves took sanctuary at the shrines of the gods. During biblical times, those who had killed someone accidentally could take asylum in cities designated for refuge.

In recent years, dozens of U.S. cities and counties became part of this tradition by adopting so-called "sanctuary policies" that bar local law enforcement from cooperating with federal immigration authorities. The policies aim to build safer communities by strengthening undocumented immigrants' trust in local police. Though the South has disproportionately fewer sanctuary communities compared to other regions, they include major cities like New Orleans and Austin, Texas.

But these sanctuary policies are now under attack at the federal and state levels.

President Donald Trump (R) signed an executive order on Jan. 25 titled "Enhancing Public Safety in the Interior of the United States" that makes all undocumented immigrants targets of deportation, citing them as "a threat to national security and public safety." The order specifically targets sanctuary cities, claiming that they cause "immeasurable harm to the American people," and threatens to deprive them of federal grants "except as deemed necessary for law enforcement purposes."

After the signing of this executive order, Florida's Miami-Dade County became the first major metro area to rescind its sanctuary city policy, with Mayor Carlos Giménez (R) instructing the county jail to honor all immigration detainer requests from the U.S. Department of Homeland Security. The mayor's actions are now being fought over in the courts.

In Texas, after Travis County Sheriff Sally Hernandez announced that her department would not comply with Immigration and Customs Enforcement (ICE) detainer requests unless federal officials had a warrant, Gov. Greg Abbott (R) cancelled $1.5 million in criminal justice grants to the county, which includes the state capital of Austin. Meanwhile, the Texas legislature is again considering legislation banning sanctuary cities, which is drawing protests.

Other Southern legislatures are also considering bills targeting sanctuary cities:

- After defeating a ban on them last year, Florida lawmakers are again considering outlawing sanctuary city policies and imposing penalties and fines on local governments that adopt them.
- North Carolina lawmakers banned local measures that limited cooperation with federal immigration officials in 2015, but there are now separate bills being considered in the state House and Senate that would raise the stakes by withholding funds from local governments with sanctuary policies.
- There's also a sanctuary city ban on the books in Tennessee, but this year legislators there introduced a bill to impose penalties on sanctuary cities. Though there are no sanctuary cities in the state, the sponsors call their measure "proactive."
- Virginia lawmakers are currently considering SB 1262, which would make any sanctuary city liable for injuries and damages caused by an "illegal alien."

And Georgia, which has had a ban on sanctuary cities since 2009, last year began requiring local governments to certify that they cooperate with federal immigration officials in order to receive state funding.

Schools, churches organize to help the undocumented

Despite these attempts to stifle sanctuaries, some local governments are refusing to cave into the political pressure.

Days after Trump signed his executive order targeting sanctuary cities, Mayor William Bell (D) of Birmingham, Alabama, declared his a "welcoming city" and said the police would not be "an enforcement arm of the federal government" with respect to immigration law. Though Birmingham's policy does not allow the city to implement ordinances that oppose federal laws, the city council unanimously passed a resolution on Jan. 31 symbolically supporting Birmingham being a sanctuary.

"Birmingham stands with immigrants," City Council President Johnathan Austin said. "Birmingham stands with our residents."

Campuses and faith communities are also standing up to protect people at risk of deportation.

Following the election of Donald Trump, student activists at dozens of universities nationwide rallied to make their campuses sanctuaries that would protect undocumented students by banning ICE agents unless they have a warrant, forbidding campus police from enforcing immigration policies, barring the gathering or disclosing of information about a student's immigration status, and offering legal support to students with immigration questions.

The presidents of Connecticut College, Portland State University and the University of Pennsylvania among others have released statements declaring their campuses to be sanctuaries. Though no Southern university has officially declared itself a sanctuary, student activists at Duke University in North Carolina, Florida State University, Texas State University, the University of Mississippi and the University of North Carolina at Chapel Hill are among those pressing their administrations to declare the schools sanctuaries.

Faith communities are also stepping up to offer sanctuary to undocumented immigrants. Drawing on the tradition of the sanctuary movement of the 1980s in which thousands of people fleeing U.S.-funded civil wars in Central America were given refuge in churches, faith-based immigrant advocates are organizing a new sanctuary movement, with participants pledging to resist the Trump administration's proposals to target and deport millions of undocumented immigrants and to open up congregations and communities as sanctuary spaces. It now involves as many as 800 faith congregations including Christians, Jews and Muslims.

While the organizers hope it is unlikely that ICE agents will enter churches, which are classified as "sensitive locations" under department policy, they say they are prepared to implement a modern Underground Railroad if necessary to transport undocumented immigrants to Canada, which has more protective refugee policies.

"If the law is unjust, you have to disobey it," said Jim Rigby, pastor of Saint Andrew's Presbyterian Church, a sanctuary congregation in Austin, Texas. "To me you're not a church if you say no. I mean, what does it mean to say that I'm Christian only up to my nation's boundary?"

"Requiring the federal government to keep track of and regularly report on the victimization of Americans by illegal aliens is not only a good idea, it is something that the American people should demand."

Crime Rates Among Illegal Immigrants Are Misrepresented

Hans A. von Spakovsky and Grant Strobl

In the following viewpoint Hans A. von Spakovsky and Grant Strobl claim that the national media is not being truthful in what it reports about sanctuary cities and the criminal activities of illegal immigrants. They cite provisions within president Trump's executive order concerning immigration and sanctuary cities that should protect immigrants who are not criminals. They also claim that crime statistics are being misrepresented or are misleading when it coms to crime rates among illegal and undocumented immigrants. They also state that requiring the federal government to keep track of and regularly report on the victimization of Americans by illegal aliens is something that the American people should demand. Hans A. von Spakovsky is a senior legal fellow for the Heritage Foundation. Grant Strobl is national chairman for Young Americans for Freedom.

"What the Media Won't Tell You About Illegal Immigration and Criminal Activity," by Hans A. von Spakovsky and Grant Strobl, The Heritage Foundation, March 13, 2017. Reprinted by permission.

As you read, consider the following questions:

1. What is it that the article authors claim the media isn't telling citizens?
2. What are some of the kinds of statistics that the authors use to prove their point?
3. What is it that the authors say Americans should demand?

Normally, the ACLU promotes transparency in government and the ability of the public to access public records. But apparently that changes when transparency might reveal damaging information that hurts their opposition to President Trump's common-sense, revised executive order temporarily suspending entry from six terrorist safe havens in the Middle East and Africa.

How else can one explain the ACLU's criticism of a little-noticed provision in the executive order that requires the Justice Department and the Department of Homeland Security to, among other things, report on the "number and types of acts of gender-based violence against women" in the U.S., like the "honor" killings committed by foreign nationals? That provision will also require public reporting on the number of foreign nationals charged/convicted of "terrorism-related offenses" or removed from the country for terrorism-related activities.

President Trump announced in his speech to Congress that the Victims of Immigration Crime Engagement office (VOICE) would help victims of crimes committed by aliens. There's also a provision in his Jan. 25 executive order directing DHS to provide "a comprehensive list of criminal actions committed by aliens" on a weekly basis. Yet the Left and the media again made the claim that aliens commit less crime than native-born citizens and that the only "cruel" purpose of these actions is to "tag immigrants as criminals."

According to a recent Associated Press article, "multiple studies have concluded that immigrants are less likely to commit crime than native-born U.S. citizens." But the issue isn't non-citizens who are in this country legally, and who must abide by the law to avoid having their visas revoked or their application for citizenship refused. The real issue is the crimes committed by illegal aliens. And in that context, the claim is quite misleading, because the "multiple studies" on crimes committed by "immigrants" — including a 2014 study by a professor from the University of Massachusetts, which is the only one cited in the article — combine the crime rates of both citizens and non-citizens, legal and illegal.

That isn't the only problem with the study. Instead of using official crime data, it uses "self-reported criminal offending and country of birth information." For obvious reasons, there is little incentive for anyone, let alone criminal aliens, to self-report "delinquent and criminal involvement." When it comes to self-reporting criminal activity, some respondents will, no doubt, exaggerate. Others will flat out lie. Furthermore, many respondents will likely not disclose if they are a non-citizen out of fear of discovery and deportation.

These claims overlook disturbing actual data on crimes committed by criminal aliens. For example, the Government Accountability Office released two unsettling reports in 2005 on criminal aliens who are in prison for committing crimes in the United States, and issued an updated report in 2011.

The first report (GAO-05-337R) found that criminal aliens (both legal and illegal) make up 27 percent of all federal prisoners. Yet according to the Center for Immigration Studies, non-citizens are only about nine percent of the nation's adult population. Thus, judging by the numbers in federal prisons alone, non-citizens commit federal crimes at three times the rate of citizens.

The findings in the second report (GAO-05-646R) are even more disturbing. This report looked at the criminal histories of 55,322 aliens that "entered the country illegally and were still illegally in the country at the time of their incarceration in federal or state prison or local jail during fiscal year 2003." Those 55,322 illegal aliens had been arrested 459,614 times, an average of 8.3 arrests per illegal alien, and had committed almost 700,000 criminal offenses, an average of roughly 12.7 offenses per illegal alien.

Out of all of the arrests, 12 percent were for violent crimes such as murder, robbery, assault and sex-related crimes; 15 percent were for burglary, larceny, theft and property damage; 24 percent were for drug offenses; and the remaining offenses were for DUI, fraud, forgery, counterfeiting, weapons, immigration, and obstruction of justice.

The 2011 GAO report wasn't much different. It looked at 251,000 criminal aliens in federal, state, and local prisons and jails. Those aliens were arrested nearly 1.7 million times for close to three million criminal offenses. Sixty-eight percent of those in federal prison and 66 percent of those in state prisons were from Mexico. Their offenses ranged from homicide and kidnapping to drugs, burglary, and larceny.

Once again, these statistics are not fully representative of crimes committed by illegal aliens: This report only reflects the criminal histories of aliens who were in prison. If there were a way to include all crimes committed by criminal aliens, the numbers would likely be higher because prosecutors often will agree to drop criminal charges against an illegal alien if they are assured that immigration authorities will deport the alien.

The GAO reports also highlight another important flaw in the study referenced by the Associated Press. It uses survey data from a nationally representative sample of people living in the United States. Thus, the study does not take into account some potentially key factors highlighted in the GAO reports: that criminal aliens from Mexico disproportionately make up incarcerations (GAO-05-337R) and that most arrests are made in the three border states of California, Texas, and Arizona (GAO-05-646R and GAO-11-187).

One 2001 study that does take country of origin and geographic concentration factors into account found that Mexican immigrants "commit between 3.5 and 5 times as many crimes as the average native." It also pointed out the large concentration of Mexican immigrants in the Southwest, which indicates that a nation-wide sample may not represent what is happening in states with a large concentration of criminal aliens.

Although there are no perfect measures of crimes committed by criminal aliens, it has certainly not been substantiated, as the Associated Press article states, that illegal aliens commit crimes at a lesser rate than either native-born or naturalized American citizens. In fact, existing data seems to show that the opposite is likely true.

But we do know one thing for sure. Every crime committed by an illegal alien is one that would not have occurred if that alien wasn't in the United States in the first place. That includes the hundreds of thousands of crimes committed by the 55,322 illegal aliens in the GAO study who victimized countless numbers of Americans.

So despite the criticism from the ACLU and others, requiring the federal government to keep track of and regularly report on the victimization of Americans by illegal aliens is not only a good idea, it is something that the American people should demand.

| "Sanctuary policies have no effect on crime rates, despite narratives to the contrary."

Immigrants Are Less Likely to Commit Crimes

Lauren Carasik

In the following viewpoint Lauren Carasik argues that that sanctuary cities' crime statistics are being misrepresented, and that these cities are actually enhancing, not underwhelming security for their citizens. The author specifies the role of sanctuary cities, which is not to harbor criminals or illegal immigrants, but simply to refuse to carry out immigration enforcement on behalf of federal immigration authorities. Lauren Carasik is Clinical Professor of Law and Director of the International Human Rights Clinic at Western New England University School of Law.

As you read, consider the following questions:

1. What are some of the arguments for and against sanctuary cities?
2. Why were the original sanctuary cities formed in the 1980s?
3. Why does President Trump need local law enforcement for immigration issues?

The furor against sanctuary cities hit a fevered pitch after the July 2015 killing of thirty-two-year-old Kathryn Steinle. She was shot in San Francisco by Juan Francisco Lopez-Sanchez, an undocumented Mexican immigrant who had seven felony convictions and had been deported five times. Lopez-Sanchez had been released when the San Francisco police declined to detain him for immigration authorities after drug charges against him were dropped.

A year later at the Republican National Convention, Donald Trump used her death as a rallying cry: "My opponent wants sanctuary cities but where was the sanctuary for Kate Steinle?" One of his first actions as president was to sign an executive order threatening to strip federal funding from sanctuary cities—an estimated four hundred jurisdictions that limit, in varying degrees, the manner in which their police assist with immigration enforcement.

Trump tells a story of recalcitrant local authorities, violent immigrants, and sanctuary cities as breeding grounds for crime. Apparently many Americans embrace that story. In recent polls, a majority oppose sanctuary cities and want local law enforcement to cooperate with federal authorities. Why then, under the threat of Trump's order, did many sanctuary cities double down on their commitments to immigrants?

While Miami mayor Carlos Gimenez acquiesced to the administration's threat and ordered his jails to comply with federal requests, other jurisdictions have reaffirmed their immigrant-friendly positions and some are considering expanding protections, such as California, which may adopt sanctuary policies statewide, and Washington, D.C., which allocated additional funding to provide legal aid to immigrants facing deportation.

Opponents of sanctuary cities see them as a blight on public safety, but security concerns are one of the reasons that hundreds of jurisdictions think sanctuary cities are a good idea. It all depends on your views of the threat of criminality among immigrants and what policies best serve public safety. Fortunately the record on those issues is well-documented.

Trump's assertion that sanctuary cities breed crime is, like many of his other canards about immigrants, unfounded. An October 2016 study by researchers from University of California, Riverside and Highline College found "no statistically discernible difference in violent crime rate, rape, or property crime across the cities." They concluded that "sanctuary policies have no effect on crime rates, despite narratives to the contrary." The report echoes the findings of other studies that do not bear out increased crime in sanctuary cities. And the societal benefits are not limited to lower crime: economies are stronger in sanctuary counties.

Moreover Trump's order, in addition to being questionably legal, will undermine, not enhance, security. Indeed one of the most critical arguments for the necessity of sanctuary cities is one of public safety: local officials cannot protect communities that do not trust them. Few if any cities refuse to turn over immigrants charged with serious offenses. Instead they balk at turning over those arrested for minor infractions or verifying the immigration status of people encountered in the course of normal policing. In other words, they simply treat immigrants the same way as everyone else. The *New York Times* points this out in its story about the Steinle case. While the tragedy was exploited to depict immigrants as dangerous criminals, Lopez-Sanchez did not have a record of violent crime. There is evidence to indicate he did not intend to commit murder, since "the bullet he fired was found to have ricocheted off the pier." And the suggestion that he sought out San Francisco because it was a sanctuary city is also false. In fact federal officials sent him there to face a minor drug charge, after which he was released—as would be anyone else with only a minor drug offense. The backstory does not ease the anguish of Steinle's family, but the grand narrative about immigrants that Trump has consistently sought to advance is simply not true. Immigration status is not a predictor of criminality. Quite the opposite: studies have shown that immigrants in the United States commit fewer crimes than native-born citizens.

Misrepresentations also abound about what sanctuary cities actually do and the nature of their commitments. Sanctuary cities take their name from the sanctuary movement that sprung up in the 1980s to provide safe haven for Central American refugees desperate to avoid deportation to the violence-stricken countries from which they fled. Many Americans saw the mayhem as a direct result of Washington's policies supporting repressive regimes in the region, which, compounded by U.S. hostility to asylum claims from Salvadorans and Guatemalans, motivated a sense of heightened duty by many houses of worship to shelter immigrants from law enforcement.

Unlike the sanctuary movement, sanctuary cities are not actively harboring the undocumented or forgiving crimes when they do commit them; they are refusing to take on tasks of federal immigration enforcement that were never theirs to begin with. Although sanctuary cities can refuse to cooperate, their ability to impede federal immigration is fairly limited: they cannot prevent federal authorities from conducting raids or otherwise enforcing immigration laws themselves.

The number of sanctuary cities grew rapidly in response to the Secure Communities program, implemented under President Bush and continued under the Obama administration. Under that program, local law enforcement sent the fingerprints of anyone arrested to a national database and often detained arrestees for immigration authorities. Numerous complaints—about the program's impact on safety, concerns about due process and racial profiling, and that it ensnared people for minor offenses as well as non-offenders—compelled the Obama administration to curtail the program in 2014. Under its successor, the Priority Enforcement Program, which focuses on immigrants thought to threaten national and border security and public safety, Immigration and Customs Enforcement (ICE) continues to be notified of all arrests.

Trump's deportation priorities vastly expand those designated by Obama, and he has ordered the reinstatement of the Secure Communities Program.

Jurisdictions have good reasons to adopt sanctuary policies, some political and some pragmatic. Some municipalities do not want local law enforcement to be active participants in mass deportation and have rallied to the defense of their immigrant communities, in part because the failure of immigration reform has made it impossible for people to stay legally and they abhor the idea of tearing communities apart. Others believe immigration enforcement should be reserved for federal authorities. But the objections extend far beyond jurisdictional and political ones. The primary one is that effective policing is predicated on community trust. The President's Task Force on 21st Century Policing recognized this: "At all levels of government, it is important that laws, policies, and practices not hinder the ability of local law enforcement to build the strong relationships necessary to public safety and community well-being." The report concludes that "whenever possible, state and local law enforcement should not be involved in immigration enforcement."

This is particularly important to protect the vulnerable, such as victims of domestic and sexual violence or exploitation. For them, the fear that interaction with law enforcement could lead to deportation bolsters the power of abusers and serves to further isolate and silence them. Last month in Texas, a woman was detained by ICE—which was acting on a tip suspected to have come from her alleged abuser—in the courthouse just after obtaining a protective order against him. Although records later showed that the woman may have had her own criminal history, the message to other victims about the risks of seeking protection is chilling. Similarly, witnesses critical to prosecuting crimes or good Samaritans may be reluctant to come forward without assurances that they do not risk being reported to immigration authorities. Compounding the cost to community trust, using police departments' resources to assist in federal immigration enforcement can drain local budgets. Facilitating deportation exacts significant social costs as well, by devastating families and losing immigrants' contributions to community.

As Republican governors threaten to cancel grants to sanctuary jurisdictions and lawmakers propose legislation banning sanctuary policies, Trump's executive order compromises the safety of communities. Its legality is also suspect.

While sanctuary cities do not conflict with federal law, there is a strong argument that punishing sanctuary cities runs afoul of the Tenth Amendment, which bars the federal government from "commandeering" state and local government to effectuate its policies, as well as spending clause restrictions. San Francisco, which has had a sanctuary law since 1989, was the first municipality to sue the Trump administration, claiming the order is unconstitutional. The city has an estimated 30,000 undocumented immigrants and risks losing $1.2 billion in federal funding. Another legal hurdle is that ICE detainers-—agency requests that local law enforcement continue to hold someone for forty-eight hours who would otherwise be released—are likely unconstitutional. As the ACLU argued, the detainers implicate the Fourth Amendment because they cause extended detention "without probable cause, without judicial approval, and without due process protections." Those arguments have already convinced some federal courts that the detainer policies are illegal, and some municipalities will not detain people for ICE without judicial oversight.

Trump's motivation in punishing resistant communities may be partly informed by the challenges he faces in carrying out the magnitude of deportations he has promised. Even with his intention to hire an additional 15,000 border enforcement and ICE agents, a plan that presents significant logistical challenges, the president needs to tap the resources of local police to achieve his deportation goals. But as with at least one other Trump immigration initiative, the administration will first have to defend its order in court.

| "What we found is that it [sanctuary policies] improves safety."

Sanctuary Cities Do Not Protect Criminals

Maura Ewing

In the following viewpoint, Maura Ewing uses examples from several real-life immigration cases to argue that, contrary to some of the information in the media, sanctuary cities do not protect immigrants from deportation, but they can delay the process, especially for immigrants who are not a security risk to their communities or the United States. Detainers and requests for notification of releases from jail are at the heart of the sanctuary city debate, since federal officials would enlist local law enforcement officials to perform those jobs, which local officials feel would erode trust in the community. Maura Ewing is a Brooklyn-based journalist whose work has appeared in The Nation and the Atlantic, among other publications.

As you read, consider the following questions:

1. Why is President Trump's definition of sanctuary misleading?
2. What kinds of protection do immigrants actually have in sanctuary cities?
3. Do sanctuary cities help immigrants who have criminal records?

"In Sanctuary Cities, Immigrants Find Themselves With Few Real Protections From Federal Officials," by Maura Ewing, PRI's The World, December 29, 2016. Reprinted by permission from PRI*.

For immigrants with a criminal record, sanctuary cities don't provide protection from deportation. They can, though, delay the process.

In Philadelphia, a year-long probe ended last month when Immigration and Customs Enforcement caught a man with convictions for manufacturing and selling illicit drugs, resisting arrest and theft. Winston Enrique Perez Pilarte, 40, is a Dominican Republic native and a green card-holding, permanent legal resident of the US. His convictions, though, make him eligible for deportation.

He was arrested last year as a suspect in a slew of crimes including attempted rape, unlawful sexual contact with a minor and aggravated indecent assault. In most cities, this arrest would have led him straight to deportation proceedings. But because Philadelphia is a so-called sanctuary city he was released from jail back to the community while his trial was pending, just as a US citizen would have been. He evaded ICE for a year before agents picked him up.

Over the past few months, mayors across the country have doubled-down on their promises to retain sanctuary city policies despite President-elect Donald Trump's promises to withhold federal funding to their cities for doing so. More jurisdictions are joining the about 300 cities, counties and states with sanctuary-like policies. Among the latest: Santa Ana, California, where the city council decided earlier this month to give the city sanctuary designation.

Broadly, sanctuary city policies limit cooperation between local law enforcement agencies and ICE. What this means on the ground, though, has been obscured by political rhetoric. As The *New York Times* editorial board noted this week: "The word 'sanctuary' as Mr. Trump deploys it — a place where immigrant criminals run amok, shielded from the long arm of federal law — is grossly misleading, because cities with 'sanctuary' policies cannot obstruct federal enforcement and do not try to."

"Sanctuary cities absolutely do not mean that the city is able to protect people from deportation," says Caitlin Barry, a professor of law at Villanova University in Philadelphia. "The policy says that city employees are not going to use their time and resources to facilitate a deportation or to facilitate the detention of someone who the city's criminal system has already decided to release."

Even in sanctuary cities, fingerprint data from arrestees is shared with the FBI, which passes the information to the Department of Homeland Security and ICE. So even if a person is not convicted of the crime for which they are arrested, undocumented immigrants with previous convictions are at risk of ICE deportation.

ICE officials in Philadelphia requested that the Philadelphia Police Department hand Pilarte over to them when he was released from jail through what is called a detainer request. But because Philadelphia is a sanctuary city, this request was not acknowledged and Pilarte was released to the community.

Detainers and requests for notification of release are at the heart of the sanctuary city debate. Advocates argue that by creating a jail-to-deportation pipeline, local police officers are turned into de-facto immigration patrols, which errodes trust between immigrants and the cities where they live.

"What we found is that it [sanctuary policies] improves safety," says Peter Pedemonti, director of New Sanctuary Movement of Philadelphia, an immigrant rights organization. "Our immigrant community is able to build trust with the city and the police as well. They feel comfortable to call when they need something."

This was the case for Estela Hernandez, 35, when her husband was robbed last year. The couple are undocumented immigrants, originally from Oaxaca, Mexico, who have been in Philadelphia for 12 years. Last winter, Hernandez's husband was walking home from a night shift at the supermarket where they both work when he was mugged. The thieves took his wallet and his ring. Because Philadelphia is a sanctuary city, Hernandez says, she felt comfortable calling the police to report the attack.

"Previously I wouldn't have called the police if there were an incident," she says, remembering being scared of the local police before former Mayor Michael Nutter enacted sanctuary policies in 2014.

In this case, the police went above and beyond what she expected, she says. Not only did they treat the couple with respect, but they also directed her husband to an immigration lawyer who could help them file for a U Visa, which is a visa for the victims of crime. They are still in the process of applying.

Another common argument in support of sanctuary cities is that it wastes local law enforcement's time and resources on a task that is out of their purview.

"The policy says that city employees are not going to use their time and resources to facilitate a deportation or to facilitate the detention of someone who the city's criminal system has already decided to release," Barry says.

Philadelphia Mayor Jim Kenney affirmed the city's status after Trump's election in November, but said they would instead call themselves a "Fourth Amendment city." (The Fourth Amendment of the Constitution requires the government to have probable cause to conduct searches, seizures or arrests.)

"We have no authority to violate the Fourth Amendment. All the immigration officials have to do is get a warrant signed by a federal magistrate and we'll be happy to turn that person over," Kenney said.

But ICE officials in Philadelphia say they are just asking for information.

"We're not asking the city of Philadelphia to do our job," says Tom Decker, field office director for ICE's Enforcement and Removal Operations in Philadelphia. "We're not asking the city of Philadelphia anything other than: 'Here is our notification, our detainer, just contact us when they're going to be released and let us do our job safely.'"

Decker says by not acknowledging its detainer requests, local agents are merely slowing down the inevitable. When a person has had a detainer request placed on them in jail, they are given a copy of it upon release. And so, "They go, they run," he says.

In the Pilarte case, ICE agents were not able to locate him in the community. They found him when he showed up for a court date last month—where ICE officials were waiting in the courtroom to take him into custody.

For documented, non-citizens, the Trump administration could increase deportations. Undocumented immigrants can be deported by ICE at any time, but those who are here legally, such as Pilarte, must be convicted of a very broadly defined "aggravated felony," which includes crimes such as filing a false tax return and failure to appear in court.

Kris Kobach, Kansas's secretary of state, was photographed coming out of a meeting with Trump earlier this month holding documents that listed policy recommendations including targeting "any alien arrested for any crime" for deportation. "Alien" is anyone who is not a citizen.

Should Trump heed this advice, sanctuary cities would need to reform the policing practices if they wanted to limit how much their work on crime intersects with immigration enforcement. They could, for example, limit so-called "broken windows policing" in New York City and stop-and-frisk in Philadelphia, which ensnare people in the criminal justice system for low-level offenses.

Max Rivlin-Nadler wrote in the *Village Voice* this month, "[F]or many residents, the promise sanctuary never arrived, until broken windows is ended or reformed, it remains a long way off."

"Sanctuary policies ... destroy the trust of the community at large that the laws will be faithfully enforced to preserve the quality of life for all."

Sanctuary Cities Threaten Public Safety

Jessica Vaughan

In the following viewpoint, Jessica Vaughan argues that contrary to the assertions made by sanctuary cities, they do not build trust between local law enforcement and immigrants, and are actually a threat to public safety. The author cites statistics and case studies from many immigration cases around the country. She also claims that the reasoning that sanctuary cities make immigrants more comfortable with reporting crimes to local police is actually a myth, and that there are no meaningful differences among ethnic groups in crime reporting. It is usually the language barrier that prevents immigrants from reporting crimes, not the fear of discovery and deportation, she writes. Jessica Vaughan is Director of Policy Studies for the Center for Immigration Studies.

As you read, consider the following questions:

1. What do sanctuary cities have to do with public trust?
2. What was President Obama's Priority Enforcement Program?
3. What is the "chilling effect"?

"Sanctuary Cities: A Threat to Public Safety," by Jessica Vaughan, Center for Immigration Studies, July 23, 2015. Reprinted by permission.

P ublic safety problems are created when local governments adopt policies that obstruct immigration enforcement, commonly known as sanctuary policies. According to ICE records, as of October 2014 there were 276 such jurisdictions in the United States. Over an eight-month period in 2014, more than 8,100 criminal aliens who were the subject of detainers were instead released back to the streets as a result of local non-cooperation policies. Approximately two-thirds of these individuals had a serious criminal history at the time of their release. Nearly 1,900 have subsequently re-offended. Only 28 percent have been re-apprehended by ICE.

Sanctuary policies do nothing to build trust between immigrant communities and local law enforcement. They do not improve access to law enforcement services for immigrants; nor have they been shown to increase the likelihood that more immigrant crime victims will report crimes. On the contrary, they destroy the trust of the community at large that the laws will be faithfully enforced to preserve the quality of life for all.

Despite widespread public outrage at the San Francisco Sheriff's policies that caused the release of a man with five prior deportations and seven felony convictions, and who was the subject of an ICE detainer, who then went on to kill Kathryn Steinle, it is clear that some jurisdictions will not budge from their criminal alien sanctuary policies. To make matters worse, the Obama administration's new Priority Enforcement Program (PEP) explicitly allows local jurisdictions to obstruct ICE – and also establishes the entire country as a sanctuary for nearly all illegal aliens by further narrowing enforcement priorities and severely restricting the ability of ICE officers to deport removable aliens, including many with criminal records. Therefore, Congress must step in to correct the situation by a) clarifying in the law that local law enforcement agencies are expected to comply with ICE detainers; b) establishing that local law enforcement agencies will have qualified immunity when cooperating in good faith; c) implementing sanctions for those jurisdictions that continue to refuse to obstruct enforcement; and d) reversing the Obama administration's non-enforcement policies.

Sanctuaries Are Not a New Problem

The Steinle case was not the first time that an illegal alien killed someone after being released back to the streets because a local law enforcement agency ignored an ICE detainer. In 2014, a man was released by the Cook County Sheriff after serving a 60-day sentence for a domestic assault conviction, despite an ICE detainer. Soon afterwards, in Romeoville, Illinois, he killed a 15-year old girl named Brianna Valle, and also shot her mother. In 2011, in Albion New York, a man was released after bonding out on burglary charges, despite an ICE detainer. He later stabbed and killed 45-year old Kathleen Byham outside a Walmart store.

Data on Rejected Detainers

Local refusal to comply with ICE detainers has become a public safety problem in many communities and a mission crisis for ICE that demands immediate attention.

According to a report1 prepared by ICE that I obtained in a FOIA request, as of October, 2014 there were 276 state and local jurisdictions that had adopted policies of non-compliance with some or all ICE detainers, or other forms of immigration enforcement obstruction, such as barring ICE from interviewing inmates in jails. These took the form of policies, laws, executive orders or regulations. These jurisdictions were located in 43 states and the District of Columbia.

Sanctuary policies are not considered mainstream law enforcement practice, by any measure. The 276 jurisdictions represent a small fraction of the more than 17,000 law enforcement jurisdictions nationwide. Nevertheless, they include jurisdictions with large populations of illegal aliens and also significant problems with a direct connection to illegal immigration, such as drug trafficking and gang crime – such as Chicago, San Francisco, New York, Philadelphia, Miami, Baltimore and Washington, DC.

Number of Detainers Refused: From January 1, 2014 to August 31, 2014, local law enforcement agencies refused to comply with a total of 8,811 detainers, resulting in their release from custody. These detainers were associated with 8,145 individuals, of whom:

- 7,600 had one declined detainer
- 464 had two declined detainers
- 81 had three or more detainers.

As of June, 2015 the total number of detainers declined by local law enforcement agencies reportedly was over 17,000.

Most Offenders Released Had Prior Arrests; One-fourth Were Already Felons: The majority (63%) of the individuals freed by local agencies had a serious prior criminal record.

- 5,132 were previously convicted or charged with a crime or were labeled a public safety concern. Of these,
- 2,984 had a prior felony conviction or charge
- 1,909 had a prior misdemeanor conviction or charge related to violence, assault, sexual abuse, DUI, weapons, or drug distribution or trafficking
- 239 had three or more other misdemeanor convictions.

The report does not state how many of the released offenders had prior single misdemeanors or other types of violations not directly associated with violence, assault or drugs.

Released Offenders Later Arrested Again: Of the 8,145 individual aliens freed by local agencies, there were 1,867 (23%) who were subsequently arrested again for a criminal offense.

- ICE took action (arrest or removal) against 40 percent (751) of the 1,867 who re-offended.
- 1,116 (60%) of the re-offenders were at large at the time of the study.

Crimes Committed After Subject's Release: The 1,867 offenders who were released and subsequently re-offended were arrested 4,298 times during the eight-month period covered by the study. They accumulated 7,491 new charges in total, after their release.

Ten percent of the new charges involved dangerous drugs and seven percent were for driving under the influence of alcohol (DUI).

The report describes six instances of very serious crimes committed by criminal alien felons who were sought by ICE with a detainer, but nevertheless released by a local law enforcement agency with sanctuary policies.

- Santa Clara County, Calif.: On April 14, 2014 an individual with nine previous convictions (including 7 felonies) and a prior removal was arrested for "first degree burglary" and "felony resisting an officer causing death or significant bodily injury." Following release, the individual was arrested for a controlled substance crime.
- Los Angeles, Calif.: On April 6, 2014 an alien was arrested for "felony continuous sexual abuse of a child." After release, the alien was arrested for "felony sodomy of a victim under 10 years old."
- San Francisco, Calif.: On March 19, 2014 an illegal alien with two prior deportations was arrested for "felony second degree robbery, felony conspiracy to commit a crime, and felony possession of a narcotic controlled substance." After release, the alien was again arrested for "felony rape with force or fear," "felony sexual penetration with force," "felony false imprisonment," witness intimidation, and other charges.
- San Mateo County, Calif.: On February 16, 2014 an individual was arrested for "felony lewd or lascivious acts with a child under 14." In addition, the alien had a prior DUI conviction. Following release by the local agency, the individual was arrested for three counts of "felony oral copulation with a victim under 10" and two counts of "felony lewd or lascivious acts with a child under 14."
- Miami Beach, Fla.: On December 19, 2013 the police department arrested an alien for felony grand theft. This alien had been ordered removed (and presumably absconded) in 2009. The alien also had prior convictions for strong-

arm robbery, cocaine possession, larceny, trespassing, theft, marijuana possession, and resisting an officer. After release by the local agency, the alien was arrested on two separate occasions; once for "aggravated assault with a weapon and larceny" and once for "under the influence of a controlled substance."

- Santa Clara County, Calif.: On November 7, 2013 an alien was arrested (and later convicted) for "felony grand theft and felony dealing with stolen property." This alien had been ordered removed in 2010 (again, a likely absconder). The alien also had prior felony and misdemeanor convictions for narcotic possession, theft, receiving stolen property, illegal entry and other crimes. After release by local authorities the alien was arrested for "felony resisting and officer causing death or severe bodily injury" and "felony first degree burglary."

Sanctuaries With the Most Releases: As of the date of the report, 276 counties in 43 states had refused to comply with an ICE detainer. The largest number of detainers were refused in the following jurisdictions:

- Santa Clara County, Calif.
- Los Angeles County, Calif.
- Alameda County, Calif.
- San Diego County, Calif.
- Miami-Dade County, Fla.

The ICE report included a list of the 20 detention facilities that had housed the inmates that were freed, but it was redacted from the document. The report states that the following jails were among the top 20:

- Santa Clara County Jail in San Jose, Calif.
- Santa Rita Jail in Dublin, Calif.
- Twin Tower Correction Facility in Los Angeles, Calif.
- Dade Correctional Facility in Miami, Fla.
- Vista Detention Facility in San Diego, Calif.

Sanctuary Policies are Based on "Chilling Effect" Myth, Not Facts

One of the most common reasons offered for non-cooperation policies is that they are needed to enable immigrants to feel comfortable reporting crimes. This frequently-heard claim has never been substantiated, and in fact has been refuted by a number of reputable studies. No evidence of a "chilling effect" from local police cooperation with ICE exists in federal or local government data or independent academic research.

It is important to remember that crime reporting can be a problem in any place, and is not confined to any one segment of the population. In fact, most crimes are not reported, regardless of the victim's immigration status or ethnicity. According to the Bureau of Justice Statistics (BJS), in 2012, only 44 percent of violent victimizations and about 54 percent of serious violent victimizations were reported to police. In 2012, the percentage of property victimizations reported to police was just 34 percent.[2]

In addition, data from the Bureau of Justice Statistics show no meaningful differences among ethnic groups in crime reporting. Overall, Hispanics are slightly more likely to report crimes. Hispanic females especially are slightly more likely than white females and more likely than Hispanic and non-Hispanic males to report violent crimes.[3] This is consistent with academic surveys finding Hispanic females to be more trusting of police than other groups.[4]

A multitude of other studies refute the notion that local-federal cooperation in immigration enforcement causes immigrants to refrain from reporting crimes:

- A major study completed in 2009 by researchers from the University of Virginia and the Police Executive Research Forum (PERF) found no decline in crime reporting by Hispanics after the implementation of a local police program to screen offenders for immigration status and to refer illegals to ICE for removal. This examination of Prince William

County, Virginia's 287(g) program is the most comprehensive study to refute the "chilling effect" theory. The study also found that the county's tough immigration policies likely resulted in a decline in certain violent crimes.[5]

- The most reputable academic survey of immigrants on crime reporting found that by far the most commonly mentioned reason for not reporting a crime was a language barrier (47 percent), followed by cultural differences (22 percent), and a lack of understanding of the U.S. criminal justice system (15 percent) — not fear of being turned over to immigration authorities. (Davis, Erez, and Avitable, 2001).

- The academic literature reveals varying attitudes and degrees of trust toward police within and among immigrant communities. Some studies have found that Central Americans may be less trusting than other groups, while others maintain that the most important factor is socio-economic status and feelings of empowerment within a community, rather than the presence or level of immigration enforcement. (See Davis and Henderson 2003 study of New York; Menjivar and Bejarano 2004 study of Phoenix).

- A 2009 study of calls for service in Collier County, Fla., found that the implementation of the 287(g) partnership program with ICE enabling local sheriff's deputies to enforce immigration laws, resulting in significantly more removals of criminal aliens, did not affect patterns of crime reporting in immigrant communities. (Collier County Sheriff's Office).

- Data from the Boston, Mass., Police Department, one of two initial pilot sites for ICE's Secure Communities program, show that in the years after the implementation of this program, which ethnic and civil liberties advocates alleged would suppress crime reporting, showed that calls for service decreased proportionately with crime rates. The precincts with larger immigrant populations had less of a decline in reporting than precincts with fewer immigrants. (Analysis of Boston Police Department data by Jessica Vaughan, 2011).

- Similarly, several years of data from the Los Angeles Police Department covering the time period of the implementation of Secure Communities and other ICE initiatives that increased arrests of aliens show that the precincts with the highest percentage foreign-born populations do not have lower crime reporting rates than precincts that are majority black, or that have a smaller foreign-born population, or that have an immigrant population that is more white than Hispanic. The crime reporting rate in Los Angeles is most affected by the amount of crime, not by race, ethnicity, or size of the foreign-born population. (Analysis of Los Angeles Police Department data by Jessica Vaughan, 2012).

- Recent studies based on polling of immigrants about whether they might or might not report crimes in the future based on hypothetical local policies for police interaction with ICE, such as one recent study entitled "Insecure Communities", by Nik Theodore of the University of Illinois, Chicago, should be considered with great caution, since they measure emotions and predict possible behavior, rather than record and analyze actual behavior of immigrants. Moreover, the Theodore study is particularly flawed because it did not compare crime reporting rates of Latinos with other ethnic groups.

For these reasons, law enforcement agencies across the country have found that the most effective ways to encourage crime reporting by immigrants and all residents are to engage in community outreach, hire personnel who speak the languages of the community, establish anonymous tip lines, and set up community sub-stations with non-uniform personnel to take inquiries and reports – not by suspending cooperation with federal immigration enforcement efforts.

Proposals to increase ICE-local cooperation, most recently the Davis-Oliver Act, which was passed by this committee, enjoy strong support among law enforcement leaders across the country. These leaders — sheriffs, police, and state agency commanders— routinely and repeatedly express concern over crime problems associated with illegal immigration and routinely and repeatedly express their willingness to assist ICE, and that it is their duty to assist ICE.[6] The National Sheriffs Association and numerous individual sheriffs and police chiefs have expressed support for the Davis-Oliver Act.

Detainer Non-cooperation Policies More Common Today

While local sanctuary policies aiming to shield illegal aliens from detection or provide access to public benefits and driver's licenses have existed for many years, the policies on rejecting detainers are a much more recent phenomenon.

As recently as 2007, the Department of Justice (DOJ) investigated the nature of sanctuary policies, and found that while a number of local jurisdictions did not go out of their way to inquire about immigration status during encounters or notify ICE of an alien in custody, nearly all jurisdictions accepted detainers at that time.[7] The DOJ audit found that 94 out of 99 (95%) jurisdictions surveyed about detainer acceptance were fully compliant. All seven of the jurisdictions that were investigated in the audit in the most detail (Oregon state corrections, New York City; San Francisco; California state corrections; Texas state corrections; Clark County, Nev.; and Cook County, Ill.) fully complied with detainers at that time. In 100 percent of the individual alien cases audited, the local agency accepted the ICE detainer.

The 2007 DOJ audit found even higher apparent recidivism rates among criminal aliens released from custody than the 2014 ICE analysis found. Looking at a four-year period after release (compared to the 8-month period covered in the 2014 ICE study), the DOJ found that 73 out of a random sample of 100 criminal aliens had re-offended after release. The aliens committed an average of six new crimes apiece after release. Noted the report: "If this data is indicative of the full population of 262,105 criminal histories [from the four-year time period], the rate at which released criminal aliens are re-arrested is extremely high."

Some jurisdictions now claim that sanctuary policies are needed because holding aliens on ICE detainers is too costly, but back in 2007, the DOJ auditors found no local agencies that had released aliens due to lack of resources.

I believe the increase in policies prohibiting compliance with all or some detainers has less to do with legitimate law enforcement concerns and more to do with the Obama administration's scheme to drastically scale back immigration enforcement.

Detainers have been used for decades and are a perfectly legitimate, lawful tool to enable ICE take custody of aliens from local authorities.[8] They help protect the public and ICE officers by allowing officers to take custody of removable aliens in a secure setting rather than on the street, in homes or at work places. The administration is pretending that it abandoned this tool because of unfavorable court rulings, but in fact top agency leaders helped instigate these rulings by reversing long-standing agency policy (over the objections of career personnel and without legal foundation) and declaring that detainers were suddenly optional for local agencies to honor. This new policy was then simply accepted by certain federal judges – leaving ICE's local law enforcement partners who had cooperated in good faith (and in compliance with federal regulations) twisting in the wind and subject to significant legal and financial liability.[9]

PEP Will Make Matters Worse

On November 20, 2014, the President announced a series of controversial executive actions, including the termination of the Secure Communities program and the establishment of a new program known as the Priority Enforcement Program (PEP). In addition to further reducing the categories and numbers of illegal aliens who will be subject to deportation, and further restricting the circumstances in which ICE officers may issue detainers or move to deport aliens, the program explicitly allows local jurisdictions to obstruct ICE by choosing to ignore ICE requests to be notified of aliens' release dates. According to Department of Homeland

Security officials, already, five of the largest jurisdictions in the country have indicated that they still will obstruct ICE and refuse to participate in PEP, not matter how much enforcement is watered down by the prioritization guidelines.

Since it is now clear that many of the sanctuaries will not reform themselves, and that the Obama administration will not move to discourage or penalize them, it is up to Congress to fix this problem.

Debarring sanctuaries from certain federal funding – specifically, debarring those jurisdictions that do not honor all ICE detainers from all law enforcement and homeland security funding – would be a reasonable interim action by Congress. But the only effective and lasting solution to local sanctuary policies would be for Congress to take multiple actions: a) clarifying in the law that local law enforcement agencies are expected to comply with ICE detainers; b) establishing that local law enforcement agencies will have qualified immunity when cooperating in good faith; c) implementing sanctions for those jurisdictions that continue to refuse to obstruct enforcement; and d) reversing the Obama administration's non-enforcement policies.

Members of Congress should beware of proposals that attempt to spell out specific criminal convictions that trigger mandatory cooperation, such as felonies, crimes of moral turpitude, or other definitions of "serious" crimes. These do more harm than good, because by distinguishing between felons and other types of aliens against whom detainers might be filed, Congress would be suggesting that it's acceptable for state and local governments to ignore detainers based on other types of immigration violations — even though the many laws laying out what constitutes a deportable offense were written and passed by Congress and signed by the president. Moreover, allowing agencies to reject detainers for aliens convicted of misdemeanors and other crimes ignores the reality that these offenders also can be a threat to public safety, in addition to being deportable. Such conditions on cooperation and enforcement will only undermine these laws and serve as an endorsement of the Obama administration's disastrous "worst of the worst only" limitations on enforcement.

In addition, distinguishing between types of detainers for immigration violations that must (or need not) be honored could expose ICE's partners to predatory litigation as a result of their cooperation. There are a number of law enforcement agencies that have been reluctant to fully honor detainers solely because they fear getting sucked into costly litigation. To address this, Congress must clarify ICE's authority to issue detainers, and provide qualified immunity for ICE's local law enforcement partners (as the law now provides for 287(g) partners).

These provisions and more are included in the Davis-Oliver Act, which has been passed by this committee. It has earned the endorsement of the National Sheriffs Association as well as many individual sheriffs and police chiefs, indicating that San Francisco Sheriff Mirkarimi's sanctuary policies and all others are well out of the mainstream of law enforcement practices in America. Congress – and the presidential candidates – should join the sheriffs' association in supporting these provisions in order to keep the list of victims from growing.

Endnotes

1 "Declined Detainer Outcome Report, ICE Law Enforcement Systems & Analysis Unit, October 4, 2014, http://cis.org/sites/cis.org/files/Declined%20detainers%20report_0.pdf.

2 Jennifer Truman, Ph.D., Lynn Langton, Ph.D., and Michael Planty, Ph.D., Bureau of Justice Statistics, "Crime Victimization 2012," http://www.bjs.gov/content/pub/pdf/cv12.pdf.

3 See additional data from the National Crime Victimization Survey here: http://www.bjs.gov/content/pub/pdf/cvus0805.pdf.

4 Lynn Langton, Marcus Berzofsky, Christopher Krebs, and Hope Smiley-McDonald, Bureau of Justice Statistics report, "Victimizations Not Reported to the Police, 2006-2010," http://www.bjs.gov/content/pub/pdf/vnrp0610.pdf.

5 Evaluation Study of Prince William County's Illegal Immigration Enforcement Policy: FINAL REPORT 2010, http://www.pwcgov.org/government/dept/police/Documents/13185.pdf.

6 See for example, the remarks of Sheriffs at these events by the Center for Immigration Studies: http://cis.org/Videos/Sanctuary-Cities-Panel, http://cis.org/Videos/Panel-Crime-Challenges, and https://cis.org/Vaughan/Sheriffs-Skeptical-Chilling-Effect-Secure-Communities

7 U.S. Department of Justice, Office of the Inspector General, Audit Report 07-07, "Cooperation Of SCAAP Recipients In The Removal Of Criminal Aliens From The United States," January, 2007, https://www.oig.justice.gov/reports/OJP/a0707/final.pdf.

8 8 USC 1226 (a) and 1357.

9 See Dan Cadman and Mark H. Metcalf, Disabling Detainers: How the Obama Administration Has Trashed a Key Immigration Enforcement Tool, Center for Immigration Studies, January, 2015: http://cis.org/disabling-detainers.

> *"When we saw that visitors to our community and our nation were under attack by this unjust position and order that the president has made, we wanted people to know that he does not speak for us."*

Sanctuary Cities Are Safer and More Community-Oriented

Alice Miranda Ollstein

In the following viewpoint, Alice Miranda Ollstein argues that President Trump's executive order, which promised to punish sanctuary cities, has not had the desired effect. Instead, more cities and towns have declared themselves to be sanctuary cities as a result of the order. Despite the threats of the loss of federal and state funding to these cities, they still maintain that sanctuary cities are more community-oriented and are fighting against civil rights violations. The author maintains that President Trump's strategy for punishing sanctuary cities has actually backfired. Alice Miranda Ollstein covers Congress, the Supreme Court, and the White House for the independent news site Talking Points Memo.

"Donald Trump Tried to Punish 'Sanctuary Cities.' It's Backfiring." by Alice Miranda Ollstein, ThinkProgress, February 2, 2017. Reprinted by permission.

As you read, consider the following questions:

1. How is President Trump trying to punish sanctuary cities?
2. What in general was the response to the president's executive order about sanctuary cities?
3. What happened in Alabama after the state passed harsh immigration laws?

P resident Donald Trump campaigned on a promise to "end" so-called sanctuary cities—jurisdictions that refuse to make their local police enforce immigration law.

"This has to end," he told a crowd in Houston in September, after talking about San Francisco's refusal to share information with federal immigration agents. "It will end if I become president, I promise you it will end."

On his fifth day in office, he signed an executive order to strip such cities and counties of their federal funding.

The threats appear to be backfiring. Since Trump's election in November, nearly a dozen cities and counties—from progressive California to deep-red Alabama—have voted to adopt sanctuary city policies. Several more cities and an entire state are considering the move. Some cities that have long held sanctuary status are taking Trump to court, while others are creating legal defense funds and taking other measures to protect undocumented residents.

"When we saw that visitors to our community and our nation were under attack by this unjust position and order that the president has made, we wanted people to know that he does not speak for us," said Jonathan Austin, the president of the Birmingham City Council, which voted unanimously this week to become a sanctuary city. "We need to be a city that's welcoming and a sanctuary to everyone, regardless of who they are."

Speaking from the other side of the country, City Council member Sal Tinajero in Santa Ana, California told ThinkProgress his city voted to declare itself a sanctuary as a direct response to Trump's election.

"The impact it was having on our families, on the psyche of our kids going to school, they were afraid of what was going to happen," he said. "We knew we had to take action before the president took his oath of office."

So far, only one sanctuary jurisdiction out of the nation's 400 or so, Miami-Dade County, has caved to Trump's defunding threat. Residents took to the streets to protest the decision, and they plan to pressure the county commission to restore sanctuary status in the weeks ahead.

A Constellation of Sanctuaries

Since Trump was elected in November, a wave of cities and counties from coast to coast have adopted the sanctuary policies Trump vowed to "end." From Birmingham, Alabama and Travis County, Texas in the deep south to Urbana, Illinois and Cincinnati, Ohio in the Midwest to Olympia, Washington and Alameda, California on the West Coast, cities large and small, urban and rural have adopted the sanctuary city label. Many, including Boulder, Colorado and Santa Ana, cited Trump's election as the motivating force for the decision.

"We were already acting as a sanctuary city with our policies, but we had not labeled ourselves a sanctuary city," Tinajero explained. "So we wanted our communities to know that we are not going to work with [Trump]. We're not going to make it easy on him."

Lansing, Michigan, Menlo Park, California, Phoenix, Arizona and Atlanta, Georgia are currently debating whether to join the list, and more cities could soon follow.

Since there is no firm legal definition of a sanctuary city, these local governments are implementing a range of practices. Some of the sanctuary resolutions have been merely symbolic and change no laws on the ground. Some ban police officers from checking the immigration status of people they stop or arrest. Some limit information-sharing and cooperation with Immigration and Customs Enforcement (ICE).

Tinajero described the delicate balance Santa Ana adopted. "Let's say, for example, that you have a person who commits a traffic violation," he said. "Our police officers will not call ICE and say, 'We have someone here who is undocumented.' We don't want people to fear that they could get pulled over one day going to work and never come back. But if people are being sought out because they committed a violent crime, that's different. We would cooperate."

The reasons officials give for making their cities into sanctuaries are as diverse as the cities themselves. Some say it's strictly a financial decision, as it's expensive for local jails to hold undocumented people until they are picked up by ICE, and they are not always reimbursed for that cost. Other cities cite public safety, arguing that if police are seen as de-facto immigration agents, undocumented residents will be afraid to come forward and report crimes.

"Local police departments work hard to build and preserve trust with all of the communities they serve, including immigrant communities," said J. Thomas Manger, the Police Chief of Montgomery County, Maryland. "Immigrants residing in our cities must be able to trust the police and all of city government. This is essential to reducing crime and helping victims."

Trump's executive order cited "aliens who engage in criminal conduct" as the rationale for cracking down on sanctuary cities, saying such people pose "a significant threat to national security and public safety." Throughout his campaign, he highlighted a handful of murders committed by undocumented immigrants as he whipped up support for his plan.

Yet a recent analysis of federal data found that sanctuary counties have lower crime rates, poverty rates, and unemployment rates than counties that fully cooperate with ICE. Overall, immigrants are much less likely to commit crimes than native-born Americans.

Other cities, including Birmingham, Alabama, presented their decision as a continuation of the struggle for civil rights.

"The city of Birmingham has always fought for justice and equality throughout our history," Austin said. "As a beacon of the civil rights movement and an example of what people can do

SANCTUARY CITIES ARE ACTUALLY SAFER

In his continued efforts to address the number of undocumented immigrants in the country, President Trump took a harder line against cities and jurisdictions whose mayors have said they won't cooperate with his plans to enlist their police forces to help the federal government round up undocumented immigrants.

The president said that he will cut federal funding to the police budgets of so-called sanctuary cities — like New York, Chicago, and Washington, D.C — which could cost them billions of dollars

But the available data on crime, immigration, and safety in cities does not support the premise for the president's actions. News outlets and researchers pointed out during the presidential campaign that immigrants who are in the country illegally are less likely to commit crimes or be incarcerated than the general population. The American Immigration Council noted in a 2015 study that the recent period of rising immigration to the United States from 1990 to 2013 also corresponded with plummeting crime rates across the country.

This past Thursday, a new study conducted Tom K. Wong, a political scientist at the University of California-San Diego, found that there are broad benefits for local jurisdictions that resist cooperating with federal immigration enforcement — they are safer in the aggregate and enjoy stronger economies. "For the first time we're kind of seeing that crime rates are lower when localities stay out of the business of federal immigration enforcement," Wong said.

He looked at federal data on immigration detainers, an ICE-initiated 48-hour hold on anyone identified as being in the country illegally. ...Wong compared the data from thousands of counties, those that ICE said did not honor detainer requests and those that did. "We don't have to make up a definition of what a sanctuary locality is," Wong said. "We have ICE telling us what it thinks a sanctuary county is."

On average, counties that did not comply with ICE requests experienced 35.5 fewer crimes per 10,000 people than those that did. Wong also found that counties that did not comply with detainer requests had higher household incomes, lower rates of unemployment, lower rates of poverty, and were less likely to have children under 18 in households receiving public benefits.

"Why Sanctuary Cities Are Safer," by Gene Demby, npr, January 29, 2017.

when they join together to combat unjust laws and policies, we have shown how to make that a reality."

In 2011, Alabama passed the harshest immigration law in the nation, requiring schools and local police officers to check the status of suspected undocumented immigrants and hand them over to federal officials. HB 56 also made it a crime to rent a house to an undocumented immigrant or even give such a person a ride. It allowed utilities companies to shut off water and electricity to people who couldn't prove their citizenship.

Tens of thousands of Latino workers fled the state, crippling several local industries and costing Alabama nearly $11 billion in tax revenue. Lawsuits from the Justice Department and civil rights groups forced the state to roll back some of the harshest provisions, and the state had to pay hundreds of thousands of dollars to residents whose rights were violated.

"There were children leaving our school system by the dozens. It impacted our agriculture and businesses across the state of Alabama," said Austin. "So we know what happens when unjust laws are put in place. And we see it again with what the president is doing now."

Austin noted that Birmingham's new sanctuary city policies, which will be developed over the next few weeks and presented to the city council, should take the fallout from HB 56 into account.

"We rely, as we have from the very beginning of this country, on immigrant labor," he said. "Not just out in the factories and fields and warehouses, but also for ideas and innovations. We need people from all walks of life working together to solve problems. So to single out a particular group of people and say, 'We don't want you,' that puts a damper on our own economy."

Federal and State-level Threats Loom

This week, San Francisco became the first sanctuary city to sue Donald Trump over his executive order that could strip away more than a billion dollars of its federal funding. "This strikes at the heart of established principles of federalism and violates the United

States Constitution," the lawsuit reads. "The executive order is a severe invasion of San Francisco's sovereignty."

Other legal experts, including attorneys at the American Civil Liberties Union, agree that the order may be unconstitutional and unenforceable.

"There is something in our Constitution called states rights," Tinajero said. "The federal government cannot coerce a state or municipality to do work that is their job, and immigration is a responsibility of the federal government. If we refuse to do it for you, you cannot then take away our funds."

If Trump moves forward with his threat to cut off federal dollars, the types of funding most at risk are grants the Justice Department and Department of Homeland Security give to states and cities to hire police officers, staff courtrooms, fund witness protection programs, provide drug treatment, and prevent domestic violence.

"That's the irony," said Tinajero. "The programs most affected are public safety and police officer programs. The National Police Officer Association supported Donald Trump, and yet he wants to take away funds and decrease their membership. That would result in a higher level of crime. I don't know if the president wants crime to escalate under his watch because of his policies."

At the same time, many Republican-controlled states are already moving aggressively on the same front—threatening to strip away state funds from sanctuary cities.

On Wednesday, Texas Gov. Greg Abbott (R) became the first to act, canceling $1.5 million in criminal justice grants to Travis County—including funding for domestic violence prevention programs and a special court for veterans. The move follows an announcement by Travis County Sheriff Sally Hernandez that her department will no longer comply with ICE requests to hold inmates suspected of being undocumented, unless ICE presents a warrant or court order.

When Abbott made the same funding threat to Dallas County in 2015, the county sheriff backed down and agreed to honor all ICE detainers. But Hernandez says she will fight back. "I will not allow fear and misinformation to be my guiding principles as a leader sworn to protect this community," she said. Abbott has also threatened to pass legislation that would allow him to remove from office Hernandez and other officials who back sanctuary policies. All 20 Republican state senators have agreed to support such a measure.

Pennsylvania Republicans introduced a bill this month to ban cities from adopting sanctuary policies, and said those that do so will lose their state grant funding. A nearly identical bill is moving forward in Idaho and Wisconsin.

Ohio Treasurer Josh Mandel (R), a rumored candidate for the Senate in 2018, has said he will do all he can to stop Cincinnati from becoming a sanctuary city. Alabama Gov. Robert Bentley (R) said he "will not support" Birmingham or any other city in the state becoming a sanctuary for immigrants, but has not yet said what he will do in response.

Periodical and Internet Sources Bibliography

The following articles have been selected to supplement the diverse views presented in this chapter.

David Bier, "Trump Is Wrong About Undocumented Immigrants and Crime." Newsweek, May 1, 2017. http://www.newsweek. com/trump-wrong-about-undocumented-immigrants-and-crime-591629

Scott Erickson, "The Truth About Sanctuary Cities and Crime Rates." February 17, 2017. https://www.cnsnews.com/commentary/scott-erickson/truth-about-sanctuary-cities-and-crime-rates

Robert Farley, "No Evidence Sanctuary Cities 'Breed Crime.'" FactCheck.org, February 10, 2017. https://www.factcheck. org/2017/02/no-evidence-sanctuary-cities-breed-crime/

Benjamin Gonzalez, Loren Collingwood, Stephen Omar El-Khatib," The Politics of Refuge: Sanctuary Cities, Crime, and Undocumented Immigration." Urban Affairs Review, May 7, 2017. http://journals.sagepub.com/doi/ abs/10.1177/1078087417704974

Christopher Ingraham, "Trump says sanctuary cities are hotbeds of crime. Data say the opposite." Washington Post, January 27, 2017. https://www.washingtonpost.com/news/wonk/wp/2017/01/27/ trump-says-sanctuary-cities-are-hotbeds-of-crime-data-say-the-opposite/?utm_term=.9111e912927c

Ron Martinelli, "The truth about crime, illegal immigrants and sanctuary cities." The Hill, April 19, 2017. http://thehill.com/ blogs/pundits-blog/crime/329589-the-truth-about-crime-illegal-immigrants-and-sanctuary-cities

Aubrey Whelan, "Philadelphia Joins Legal Backlash Against Trump's 'Sanctuary Cities' Policy." Governing.com, August 31, 2017. http://www.governing.com/topics/public-justice-safety/tns-philadelphia-trump-sessions-sanctuary-cities-lawsuit.html

Tom K. Wong, "The Effects of Sanctuary Policies on Crime and the Economy." Center for American Progress, January 26, 2017. https://www.americanprogress.org/issues/immigration/ reports/2017/01/26/297366/the-effects-of-sanctuary-policies-on-crime-and-the-economy/

OPPOSING VIEWPOINTS® SERIES

CHAPTER 3

Do Sanctuary Cities Undermine National Security?

Chapter Preface

A nother major issue that opponents and critics of sanctuary cities frequently use is that of national security. In a global society of terrorist groups who conduct attacks on public places and target innocent civilians, there is a real fear that terrorists and their supporters will find a way to infiltrate the United States and cause even more terrorist acts. Groups like al-Qaeda and ISIS are frequently in the news, and have claimed responsibility for many terrorist acts even when they have not been involved. The resulting culture of fear makes many Americans afraid that terrorist are slipping in the country as illegal or undocumented immigrants, or using tourist or student visas to gain entry. They then fear that these terrorists will take up residence in sanctuary cities and be able to do whatever they want without fear of discovery or deportation. This becomes a national security issue because the government will not be able to sufficiently police immigrants entering the US, or prosecute and deport them if they are "hiding" in safe cities.

Advocates of sanctuary cities argue that terrorist are just as likely to be American citizens who have developed sympathies for terrorist organizations. President Trump's January 2017 executive order, which banned citizens from what he named as key Muslim nations where terrorist groups are prevalent: Iraq, Syria, Iran, Libya, Somalia, Sudan, and Yemen. The order stated:

> In order to protect Americans, the United States must ensure that those admitted to this country do not bear hostile attitudes toward it and its founding principles. The United States cannot, and should not, admit those who do not support the Constitution, or those who would place violent ideologies over American law. In addition, the United States should not admit those who engage in acts of bigotry or hatred (including "honor" killings, other forms of violence against women, or the persecution of those who practice religions different from their own) or those who would oppress Americans of any race, gender, or sexual orientation.[1]

The order wreaked havoc at US airports and points of entry, as many people from these countries with legitimate visas were left stranded. The order was temporarily lifted, but has resurfaced in other iterations. President Trump has also indicated that he will build a border wall between the US and Mexico to lessen the flow of illegal immigrants from that country.

National security will continue to be one of the biggest issues in the sanctuary cities debate. Both sides have valid arguments—the safety and security of US citizens versus the ability of immigrants to escape desperate situations and find security in a new country—but ultimately the decision rests with federal and state governments.

Endnotes

1. "Executive Order Protecting the Nation from Foreign Terrorist Entry into the United States." The White House, January 27, 2017. Web. https://www.whitehouse.gov/presidential-actions/executive-order-protecting-nation-foreign-terrorist-entry-united-states/

"Every year, the U.S. government allows approximately 1 million immigrants to establish legal permanent residence in the U.S. This includes people from countries that represent a national security threat to the U.S."

Giving Illegal Immigrants Refuge Is Unfair to Those Who Came Here Legally

James Simpson

In the following viewpoint, James Simpson claims that the left-wing individuals and organizations who create funding grants are providing money aimed at overwhelming the United States with immigrants. He argues that the United States allows about 1 million immigrants, including many from countries that represent a security threat to the US, into the country, but that many more enter illegally. The author goes on to profile many organizations that, in different ways, stand to profit from allowing illegal and undocumented immigrants into the United States. James Simpson is an investigative journalist and former economist and budget examiner for the White House Office of Management and Budget.

"Refugee Resettlement: The Lucrative Business of Serving Immigrants," by James Simpson, Capital Research Center, July 28, 2015. Reprinted with permission from Capital Research Center.

As you read, consider the following questions:

1. Why can immigration issues be "lucrative" for some people and organizations?
2. What is the relationship between foundations, immigrants, and money?
3 What do government refugee contractors do?

L eft-wing grant-makers have embarked on a campaign aimed at overwhelming America with unprecedented levels of immigration. These foundations underwrite a universe of liberal organizations that are devoted to bringing in ever more people from all over the world, and the organizations' motives include money. These groups, known as "Volunteer Agencies" (VOLAGs), don't just receive private dollars from liberal foundations; they also are richly rewarded with your tax dollars when they collaborate with federal government agencies.

Every year, the U.S. government allows approximately 1 million immigrants to establish legal permanent residence in the U.S. This includes people from countries that represent a national security threat to the U.S. About 140,000 emigrate lawfully from majority-Muslim countries and an even greater number do so from the communist countries that still remain –including Cuba and China– more than two decades after the collapse of the Soviet bloc. Far more immigrants come to America illegally. Last year, almost 140,000 youths and families were welcomed into the U.S. after illegally entering the country through the Southwest border.

But these numbers aren't high enough to please the foundations that will be profiled in this study.

The Refugee Program
There is another category of newcomer that most Americans have overlooked while our country is distracted by the wave of illegal immigration. This group is having a profound impact on

the complexion of our society and is rapidly rising to the level of national security threat.

The group to which I refer are refugees from countries with bloody conflicts. Approximately 3.9 million Syrians have fled civil war and are holed up in refugee camps in surrounding countries. To date, only 700 have been resettled in the U.S., but this may change. On May 21, 14 U.S. senators signed a letter urging President Obama to expand the refugee program to allow 65,000 Syrian refugees into the U.S. by the end of 2016. This would require either a dramatic increase in the current 70,000 annual cap on all refugees, or a policy decision that would force persons from other countries to take a back seat to Syrians.

Because of the chaos in Syria, it will be virtually impossible to vet these people, according to the FBI. How many will be members of ISIS or some other terrorist group? Since ISIS members may already be here; there is little doubt more will come.

A plethora of special programs allow persons into America outside the usual immigration process, including "diversity" visas, the refugee program, asylum seekers (asylees) and their families ("follow to join"). Refugees from Iraq and Afghanistan have their own special program, Special Immigrant Visas (SIV).

Additionally, special programs allow about 20,000 Cubans and Haitians to emigrate to the U.S. annually, with the same benefits received by refugees and asylees. There is even a "Rainbow Welcome Initiative" that funds a nonprofit contractor (Heartland Alliance International, LLC) to meet the special needs of lesbian, gay, bisexual, and transgendered (LGBT) refugees and asylees. Government funds 87 percent of the $10 million nonprofit. CEO Sid Mohn makes $330,000 per year in pay and benefits according to Heartland's 2014 tax return. Combined, the top four officers receive about $850,000 per year—almost all on the taxpayer.

Finally, in 1991, the government created "Temporary Protected Status" to grant legal status in the U.S. to Salvadoran illegal aliens and others fleeing war or natural disaster in Central America. Currently, over 300,000 TPS aliens in the U.S. are entitled to all the benefits of other legal permanent residents. While they are supposed to be "temporary," TPS enrollees simply re-enroll when their status expires. Most have been here since the 1990s.

In December 2013, the Obama administration announced an in-country refugee program for Central American Minors (CAMs) that allows persons under 21 years of age from Honduras, Guatemala, and El Salvador direct travel to the U.S. While those countries tragically suffer from high crime and poor economic conditions, merely being a member of an afflicted population does not raise a person to the definition of "refugee." By offering this status, the Obama administration is deliberately expanding the definition, an action that has been called a "rogue family reunification program."

Major Foundation Supporters

Primary funding for the VOLAGs comes from the federal and state governments. But many secondary immigrant/refugee advocacy and assistance organizations are supported by wealthy state and national foundations whose assets total tens, if not hundreds, of billions of dollars. Most of these well-established foundations are the Left's primary source of support outside government. Below is a sampling of noteworthy radical-Left foundations supporting the immigrant/refugee effort.

Bauman Foundation

Grantees include a who's who of the radical Left. Director Patricia Bauman is a trust-fund leftist, also involved in other major radical left operations such as Catalist, which J. Christian Adams has called "Obama's database for fundamentally transforming America," Democracy Alliance, and the Brennan Center for Justice. She also advises J Street, the Soros-created Astroturf pro-Palestinian "Jewish" group. (The Bauman Foundation had 2014 net assets of $84 million; for more, see Foundation Watch, December 2014.)

Ford Foundation

Financed creation of the open borders movement and multiculturalism in the 1960s. Funded creation and growth of the radical Mexican American Legal Defense and Education Fund (MALDEF), which spawned the DREAM Act concept, the National Council of La Raza (NCLR) and the Puerto Rican Legal Defense and Education Fund, which gave us Supreme Court Justice Sonya Sotomayor. It is credited with turning the League of United Latin American Citizens (LULAC) from a conservative group that helped Hispanics assimilate into just another radical leftist Hispanic grievance group. Ford's impact on immigration activism cannot be overstated. (2013 net assets, $12.1 billion)

Gill Foundation

Founded by software billionaire Tom Gill, who along with Pat Stryker, another Colorado-based billionaire, provided most of the funding for the "Colorado Miracle" which turned the then-solidly Republican state Democrat blue in the 2004 and 2008 elections. Their effort was dubbed The Blueprint by authors Rob Witwer and Adam Schrager (who wrote a book with that name), and in 2005 it provided a template for the secretive left-wing funding cabal known as the Democracy Alliance. Gill supports Welcoming America organizations in Colorado, Tennessee, and Oregon. (2013 net assets, $234.4 million; for more on the Colorado Miracle, see Organization Trends, July 2013.)

Open Society Institute/Foundations

Through his philanthropies, anti-American hedge fund manager George Soros funds hundreds of radical nonprofits and causes. Soros is a major open borders advocate. From 2010 to 2013, Soros's Open Society Institute provided $1.7 million to the National Partnership for New Americans (OSI 2013 net assets, $953.7 million). Soros's Foundation to Promote Open Society had net assets $2.5 billion in 2013. The Soros Fund Charitable Foundation had 2013 net assets of $280 million. The Baltimore Open Society Institute (a.k.a. Alliance for Open Society International) had 2013 net assets of $2.4 million.

Public Welfare Foundation

A well-connected, long-established D.C.-based fund, PWF generously services a who's who of the radical Left, including the Tides Center, ACLU, Van Jones's Color of Change, the Marxist newspaper *In These Times*, the radical-left Economic Policy Institute, the Blue Green Alliance (which is the renamed Apollo Alliance, a shady group of labor, environment, Democratic Party representatives who wrote Obama's stimulus), the Center for American Progress, and many more. (2013 net assets, $488 million) PWF president Mary McClymont previously served as board chair for the Migration Policy Center, national director for legalization at the Migration and Refugee Services of the U.S. Catholic Conference, president and chief executive officer of InterAction, the largest alliance of U.S.-based international development and humanitarian nongovernmental organizations (dedicated to the U.N.'s Sustainable Development agenda), various positions with the Ford Foundation, and trial attorney for the U.S. Department of Justice's Civil Rights Division. She is the co-founder of Grantmakers Concerned with Immigrants and Refugees; chaired the board of the Migration Policy Institute; and served on the boards of Physicians for Human Rights, Amnesty International, the Advisory Committee of Elma Philanthropies Services, and the Advisory Committee on Voluntary Foreign Aid, U.S. Agency for International Development. Currently, she serves on the board of the Washington Regional Association of Grantmakers and the advisory board of New Perimeter, a global pro bono initiative of the law firm DLA Piper.

NEO Philanthropy

Formerly called Public Interest Projects, NEO spent $15.7 million in 2013 to "promote strongly aligned and effective immigrant rights organizations working to advance immigration policy and reform; immigrant civil engagement and integration; and defense of immigrant rights." This includes Alabama Appleseed ($50,000), Arab Community Center ($100,000), Border Action Network ($125,000), Border Network for Human Rights ($390,000), CASA de Maryland ($270,000), Colorado Immigrant Rights Coalition ($360,725), Comunidades Unidas ($15,000), Welcoming America ($89,000), TIRRC ($469,000), Massachusetts Immigrant and Refugee Advocacy Coalition ($210,000) and many others. Board member Patricia Bauman is the director of the Bauman Foundation. (NEO 2013 net assets, $19.6 million)

New World Foundation
Established in 1954, NWF operates as a national community foundation, bragging that "our grantmaking programs have become collaborative funds." Its goal: "build a progressive new majority for America..." Board member Don Hazenis is the former publisher of *Mother Jones* and the current editor of AlterNet and the Independent Media Institute, both far-Left media organizations. NWF president Colin Greer joined the secretive Soros machine, Democracy Alliance, in 2014. NWF board chairman Kent Wong is director of the UCLA Labor Center, vice president of the California Federation of Teachers, and a former SEIU attorney. Board member Sofia Campos, when a UCLA undergraduate, taught that school's first "Undocumented Student Experience" seminar and organized with the California DREAM Act, the federal DREAM Act, and the Right to Dream campaigns. She serves as board chair of United We Dream, "the first and largest network of undocumented immigrant youth." (2013 NWF assets, $29 million)

Unbound Philanthropy
Claims it is dedicated to "Welcoming newcomers. Strengthening communities." Its mission is to "transform long-standing but solvable barriers to the human rights of migrants and refugees and their integration into host societies...." Grant recipients include the National Immigration Forum, National Immigration Law Center, American Immigration Council, Tennessee Immigrant and Refugee Rights Coalition, Media Matters, Tides Foundation,

the radical-left Southern Poverty Law Center, and Hillary Clinton's favorite think tank: the Center for American Progress. Unbound financed the pro-refugee propaganda film Welcome to Shelbyville. Since 2008, Unbound has provided at least $2.4 million to the International Rescue Committee (IRC), and its net assets in 2013 were $141 million.

Vanguard Charitable Endowment Program
Vanguard offers customers donor-advised funds, which allow customers to channel donations to organizations of the donor's choosing, although in practice directors of donor-advised funds often recommend organizations and initiatives to support. Donor-advised funds are also often used by foundations that wish to mask their money flows to controversial grantees. Thus Vanguard has been the conduit for extensive support of immigration "reform" groups like Welcoming America. It provided over $22 million to the International Rescue Committee between 2005 and 2013. (2014 net assets $4.5 billion)

Y&H Soda Foundation
Says its mission is to support "nonprofit and Catholic organizations committed to the full participation and prosperity of the underserved in Alameda and Contra Costa Counties," which are located in eastern San Francisco Bay. Y&H Soda has provided $155,000 to welcoming projects in California since 2011; it has also funded numerous other local immigrant organizations, including the International Institute of the Bay Area (IIBA), which has its own "Immigrant Voices" program. The most prominent is East Bay Sanctuary Covenant, which claims to be "the largest affirmative asylum program in the country," representing over 500 asylum applicants per year. Through the Tides Center, Y&H has supported the Arab Resource and Organizing Center. AROC provides legal and refugee/asylum application assistance to Bay area Muslims. Y&H donated about $500,000 in 2012 to its various immigration projects. (2013 net assets, $129 million)

Reynolds Legacy

The Mary Reynolds-Babcock Foundation and the Z. Smith Reynolds Foundation of North Carolina are legacies of the Reynolds Tobacco and Aluminum fortunes, and both fund radical-Left agendas and organizations throughout the U.S. The Babcock Foundation, for example, has provided funds for numerous Welcoming America sponsors. (2013 assets, $182.4 million; Z. Smith Reynolds was profiled in Foundation Watch, June 2013)

Tides Foundation

The notorious Tides is a pass-through fund which launders money for wealthy donors who want to support radical causes without being identified. R.J. Reynolds' granddaughter, Nancy Jane Lehman, co-founded Tides in San Francisco along with New Left organizer Drummond Pike (2013 net assets, $142.3 million). Its sister organization, the Tides Center, was directed for years by ACORN founder and director Wade Rathke (2013 nets assets, $68.2 million). Tides Center lists "support to resettle displaced Iraqi refugees" and to combat "inhumane immigration policy…" among its 2013 activities. Related organizations include the Tides Network (2013 revenues, $13.7 million), Tides, Inc. (2013 net assets, $432,000), and Tides Two Rivers Fund.

Arca Foundation

This left-wing donor, based in Washington, D.C., features prominently in the radical Left's immigration agenda. Founded by Nancy Susan Reynolds, who was Nancy Jane Lehman's mother and R.J. Reynolds' youngest daughter, it funds such groups as the Tides Foundation, Center for American Progress, Demos, Media Matters for America, the Soros-created Jewish Astroturf organization J Street—which poses as a Jewish group but advocates the Palestinian cause—and the National Iranian American Council, which Robert Spencer calls "the Mullah's Mouthpiece." (2013 net assets, $55.7 million; profiled in Foundation Watch, October 2011)

Refugee Contractors

The federal government pays nine primary national contractors to resettle refugees and asylees. These voluntary agencies or VOLAGs are listed below with their initialisms:

CWS: Church World Service

ECDC: Ethiopian Community Development Council

HIAS: Hebrew Immigrant Aid Society

IRC: International Rescue Committee

LIRS: Lutheran Immigration and Refugee Services

CC/USCCB: Catholic Charities/U.S. Conference of Catholic Bishops

USCRI: U.S. Committee for Refugees and Immigrants

EMM: Episcopal Migration Ministries

WRI: World Relief Inc.

There are 350 federal subcontractors in 190 cities, all affiliated with the nine main refugee VOLAGs, but cataloging them is beyond the scope of this paper.

Because they are non-governmental organizations (NGOs), they can and do lobby for advantageous changes to immigration law and build allies in Congress and the bureaucracy, all fertilized by an open spigot of taxpayer dollars. While six of the nine contractors are affiliated with religious groups, the false notion that they are charitable organizations just doing the Lord's work needs to be corrected. They are federal contractors, relying on the government for most, and sometimes all, of their income. This is big business. They do the government's bidding, whether it honors religious principles or not.

Furthermore, the denominations represented all promote left-wing policies. Many reflect the "Social Gospel" i.e. the effort to marry socialist ideas with Christian doctrine begun by "Progressives" at the turn of the last century. Many are directly or indirectly connected to communists and communist ideas like so-called "liberation theology," which was a KGB creation according to former Romanian intelligence chief Ion Pacepa in his book *Disinformation*.

VOLAG Profiles

Church World Service

CWS is a subsidiary of the National Council of Churches, which was formed in 1950 from the Federal Council of Churches, which was often accused of being a communist front group. The Federal Council was one of the early promoters of social gospel. That tradition was carried forward by the National Council of Churches, where socialist ideology found a natural home.

NCC president Jim Winkler is a typical radical leftist. He called for impeachment of President Bush in 2006. He co-chaired the board of Healthcare Now! with Steelworkers' president Leo Gerard, who advocated violence against Tea Partiers, and the socialist Quentin Young. Young was Obama's personal physician for 20 years and his mentor on single-payer healthcare.

In addition to revenue streams from government, Church World Service has received funding from Soros, Ford, Tides, the Vanguard Fund, and many others.

Catholic Charities/U.S. Conference of Catholic Bishops

These nominally Catholic organizations are the largest VOLAGs, with hundreds of offices spread throughout the country. They are prominent members of the open borders/amnesty movement. The Catholic Campaign for Human Development (CCHD) is "the domestic anti-poverty program of the U.S. Catholic Bishops" and a grant-making vehicle of the USCCB. It was founded in Chicago in 1969 with the help of radical organizer Saul Alinsky, specifically to fund Alinsky's Industrial Areas Foundation. CCHD has been a radical leftist funding vehicle ever since, giving millions to ACORN, the radical training school Midwest Academy, and others. The Industrial Areas Foundation, where a young Barack Obama was trained in "community organizing" with financial support from the Chicago Archdiocese, receives the largest percentage of CCHD grants of any CCHD grantee.

President Obama had this to say about CCHD:

I got my start as a community organizer working with mostly Catholic parishes on the Southside of Chicago that were struggling because the steel plants had closed. The Campaign for Human Development helped fund the project and so, very early on, my career was intertwined with the belief in social justice that is so strong in the Church.

USCCB founded the Catholic Legal Immigration Network Inc., a $7 million subsidiary which assists illegal aliens based on "the Gospel value of welcoming the stranger." It aggressively promotes amnesty, believing that "all goods of the earth belong to all people. When persons cannot find employment in their country of origin to support themselves and their families, they have a right to find work elsewhere in order to survive. Sovereign nations should provide ways to accommodate this right." USCCB has 270 field offices in 47 states. Board members include Donald D. Taylor, president of the extreme-left union UNITE HERE!

Hebrew Immigrant Aid Society

HIAS describes itself as a "major implementing partner of the United Nations Refugee Agency and the U.S. Department of State." HIAS claims to be the oldest refugee resettlement agency in the world. It provides pro bono legal services for asylum applications and removal hearings. Services include "Filings with USCIS, Representation at Asylum Interviews (Credible Fear Interviews, Reasonable Fear Interviews), Representation before the Immigration Court, Representation before the Board of Immigration Appeals (BIA), and Federal court appeals." HIAS lists its values as "Welcoming, Dignity and Respect, Empowerment, Excellence and Innovation, Collaboration and Teamwork, and Accountability."

HIAS President Mark Hetfield is credited with transforming HIAS from a small agency focused on Jewish immigrants to "a global agency assisting refugees of all faiths and ethnicities." Donors include Vanguard and Tides Foundation.

International Rescue Committee

IRC is run by British Labour Party politician, David Miliband. His brother, "Red Ed" Miliband, Labour's pick for prime minister, lost in the United Kingdom's most recent election. Miliband's father was a hardcore Marxist. While Miliband distanced himself from his father's extremist views, the apple doesn't fall far from the tree. As environment minister in Tony Blair's Labour government, David Miliband turned global warming into a primary policy agenda, seeking to make all private homes "carbon neutral" and requiring nanny-state compliance inspections. He warned British citizens that having "energy inefficient homes" would become "painful" for them.

Miliband advocates raising the refugee cap above 70,000 and resettling 65,000 Syrians in the U.S., despite the impossible task of vetting them all for possible terrorist ties. Miliband earns a cool $500,000 for his "rescue" work.

IRC and Miliband have friends in George Soros, the Clintons, and U.S. Ambassador to the United Nations Samantha Power. Among its other support, IRC has received $1.2 million from George Soros's philanthropies and $2 million from the Ford Foundation over the past decade.

World Relief Inc.

Initially founded in 1947 as War Relief of the National Association of Evangelicals to address humanitarian needs of post-war Europe, it was renamed World Relief in 1950. WRI is the largest evangelical refugee resettlement agency in America. It serves in "education, health, child development, agriculture, food security, anti-trafficking, immigrant services, micro-enterprise, disaster response and refugee resettlement." In fiscal 2014, WRI dedicated about 62 percent of program revenues ($32 million) to resettling and providing extended services to 13,508 refugees and legal assistance to 11,000 immigrants. In keeping with Obama's "Welcoming" agenda, WRI has submitted its contribution in the form of a free PDF, "Welcoming the Stranger." (It is available at http://welcomingthestranger.com.)

World Relief obtains 70 percent of its funding through government contracts. Private foundation supporters include the Vanguard Charitable Foundation, Mustard Seed Foundation, Soros Fund Charitable Foundation, Pfizer Foundation, Global Impact and many others.

Lutheran Immigration and Refugee Service

LIRS has been involved in refugee resettlement for decades. Its most recent publicly available IRS filing lists 17 Lutheran and many unrelated facilities nationwide receiving refugee resettlement grants from LIRS. Both HIAS and Catholic Charities are listed as grant recipients, so apparently these organizations cross-pollinate. In addition to refugee resettlement, LIRS has been actively involved in processing what the immigration industry calls UACs (unaccompanied alien children).

LIRS CEO Linda Hartke served as chief-of-staff to former U.S. Rep. Chester Atkins (D-Mass.) in the 1990s. She later took positions with Church World Service and on National Council of Church's board of directors. Her most recent post was director of the Geneva-based Ecumenical Advocacy Alliance. Hartke wants LIRS to help create "communities of welcome" for illegal immigrants and refugees. She earns $228,000 in pay and benefits, according to IRS filings.

U.S. Committee for Refugees and Immigrants

USCRI formed as the International Institute in 1911, a brainchild of the YWCA, and became a VOLAG in 1977. Today, USCRI has 29 partner offices in 23 states dedicated to the needs of refugees and immigrants. It receives about 90 percent of revenue from government contracts. USCRI takes credit for inspiring the Obama administration's new Central American Minors program.

President and chief executive officer Lavinia Limón typifies the revolving door among VOLAG leaders. Limón served as the director of the Office of Refugee Resettlement during the Clinton administration. She then moved to the National Immigration Forum. Limón earns about $300,000 per year as CEO, according to USCRI tax filings.

Episcopal Migration Ministries
Officially known as the Domestic and Foreign Missionary Society of the Protestant Episcopal Church USA, EMM invokes the "welcoming" mantra by listing its first order of business as welcoming services. "Episcopal Migration Ministries' affiliate partners provide refugees with the information and services they require to thrive in their new communities within just months after arriving."

EMM does not provide nonprofit tax returns so the proportion of its budged received from government is not known, but since 2008, EMM has received $105.2 million from the federal government for its refugee/immigrant work.

Ethiopian Community Development Council
The smallest of the VOLAGs, ECDC received $16.3 million from government contracts in 2014, 93 percent of its total revenues. In addition, ECDC has received donations from the Open Society Institute, Komen Foundation, the United Way, Tides Foundation, even Citi Foundation (CitiBank), and others.

ECDC testified before Congress last year that the Unaccompanied Alien Children crisis could "lead to the demise of the refugee resettlement program as we know it." This was primarily a funding concern, given that virtually all of ECDC's revenue comes from government contracts.

ECDC provides a wide variety of services to refugees, and is involved in other contractual services as well, for example Small Business Administration microloans for new minority businesses.

Conclusion
All these groups like to discuss issues of immigration in terms of pure altruism, generosity, and welcoming the stranger. For some reason, they rarely if ever mention the possibility that politicians

may have self-interested motives for supporting high levels of immigration with little oversight. Much less do the groups mention that they themselves have found that by generously welcoming strangers to our land, they can receive bountiful subsidies of tax dollars that underwrite hefty salaries for persons who claim to act only from the most selfless motives.

James Simpson is an economist, businessman, and freelance writer. His writings have been published in Accuracy in Media, American Thinker, Big Government, Washington Times, WorldNetDaily, FrontPage Magazine, and elsewhere. This article was based on a short book by Simpson, The Red Green Axis: Refugees, Immigration and the Agenda to Erase America, published last month by Center for Security Policy Press.

"Today a staggering 65.3 million refugees around the globe seek a permanent home. Most reside in camps marked by disease, neglect and hopelessness."

Illegal Immigrants Were Desperate to Flee Their Conditions

Chris Welzenbach

In the following viewpoint, Chris Welzenbach profiles the World Relief organization, and specifically the offices located in the Midwest, which supports newly arrived immigrants to the United States. World Relief's funding has dropped and several of its offices have been closed, partly because of the harsh restrictions placed on immigration by President Trump's executive order barring immigrants from seven predominantly Muslim countries. The article describes the conditions that many of these refugees and immigrants are fleeing from, and underlines the new threats that they are now facing from new government policies. Chris Welzenbach is a playwright ("Downsize") who for many years was a member of Walkabout Theater in Chicago.

"The Plight of the "Other": Immigrants and Refugees in America's Heartland," by Chris Welzenbach, CounterPunch, June 9, 2017. Reprinted by permission.

As you read, consider the following questions:

1. Why does World Relief face "an uncertain future"?
2. What does World Relief do, and what types of immigrants do they serve?
3. What restrictions and possible situations do green card holders face?

Amy Rowell is the Director of World Relief for the Quad Cities (Rock Island and Moline in Illinois; Davenport and Bettendorf in Iowa). The agency Rowell runs is headquartered in Moline and receives much of its funding through the United States Refugee Admissions Program (USRAP). Today World Relief faces an uncertain future.

In 2015 and 2016, as result of the refugee crisis triggered by violence in Syria, President Obama raised the number of immigrants and refugees allowed into the country to 110,000 annually. In October 2016 the number was cut to 50,000. World Relief's funding, which is contingent on that number, has been cut proportionally. In the past, World Relief assisted 220 newly arrived refugees annually. This year that number has been slashed to 110. Five World Relief offices nationally have been shuttered.

Donald Trump's campaign famously capitalized on fear of the "other": of those who speak a different language or worship on a different day of the week—those who are not "true" Americans. Trump's promises to bar refugees from Muslim countries and round up 13 million undocumented workers were initially considered campaign bluster rather than concrete proposals. This perception has changed.

President Trump's Second Executive Order on Immigration (signed March 6, 2017) seeks to ban immigrants from Sudan, Syria, Iran, Libya, Somalia and Yemen, and would also suspend all USRAP funding for 120 days. Terrorism is cited as justification for these harsh actions that explicitly target the most vulnerable members of the world community. This Order is pending, and awaits action by the courts.

The Quad Cities are home to a substantial number of immigrants and refugees. Census figures show that 8% of the population of Rock Island County in Illinois and 13.2% of Scott County in Iowa are foreign born (some 40,000 people). Most of these newcomers hail from Mexico and Central America.

The United Nations High Commissioner on Refugees (UNHCR), headquartered in Geneva, Switzerland defines a refugee as: "someone who has been forced to flee his or her country because of persecution, war, or violence. A refugee has a well-founded fear of persecution for reasons of race, religion, nationality, political opinion or membership in a particular social group".

World Relief is in the specific business of assisting refugees who arrive here by legal means and meet UNHCR criteria. One large group of refugees is from the Democratic Republic of the Congo, where savage internecine fighting has forced tens of thousands to flee their homes. Refugees from Burma, Ethiopia, Eritrea, Iraq, Somalia and Sudan have also relocated here.

World Relief aids newly arrived refugees through programs that offer income assistance and help them receive food stamps. Other programs assist with employment and housing, and help refugees apply for citizenship. Staff members speak eight different languages, and the organization coordinates with Black Hawk College to provide English as a second language classes. World Relief also works closely with a number of area churches.

Rowell tells me her organization "walks alongside" a church group for a year, to familiarize them with the process and to help them negotiate a wilderness of government agencies and bureaucracies. Catholic Charities, Lutheran Social Services and numerous other religious entities are part of the mix.

Rowell worries that funding cuts may doom World Relief's reunification program, which seeks to keep refugee families together. "If they close down the Moline office," she tells me, "there won't be any program in the area to assist these people."

Today a staggering 65.3 million refugees around the globe seek a permanent home. Most reside in camps marked by disease, neglect and hopelessness. George Chiang came to this country from Myanmar (Burma) in 2011 after spending 20 years at a refugee camp in Thailand. He is the founder and president of the Buddhist Association of the Quad Cities, an organization of primarily Karen Burmese residing on both sides of the Mississippi.

Burma has for decades been under the thumb of a brutal military dictatorship. Those who participate in political activity there can, if discovered, face prison terms of 20 to 40 years. Military insurrection is a capital offense. Relatives of anyone raising arms against the dictatorship are also marked for death. Most of those in Chiang's organization face execution in their native land.

Displaced persons fleeing Burma must spend a minimum of five years in a Thai refugee camp before they become eligible for refugee status. Thereafter they can relocate to host nations such as Australia, New Zealand, Japan, Canada, the United States and elsewhere.

George Chiang and his Burmese compatriots represent an extreme example of the persecution, fear that drive human beings from one part of the world to another in their desperate search for sanctuary.

Rowell's organization provides initial assistance to newly arrived refugees. Thereafter a variety of other groups help these newscomers transition to their new lives in America. Quad Cities Alliance for Immigrants & Refugees (QCAIR) is one such organization.

Founded in 2012, QCAIR is an all-volunteer non-profit based in Rock Island that seeks to "bring immigrants, refugees, and other community members together, and help immigrants and refugees settle in to their new homes". QCAIR focuses on issues such as employment, relations with the police, housing and education, and hopes to assist 1,000 immigrants/refugees during the current fiscal year.

Nana Ouro-Agoro of QCAIR lists some of the issues facing newly arrived refugees: "The pace of living here is very stressful.

There is no family, no familiar support system. They don't know about bank cards and PIN numbers. They must learn how to budget. They don't know about insurance or how to fill out a tax return. They need to drive cars. They must adapt to new foods and they must learn a new language."

The lives of both refugees and immigrants have been jeopardized by Trump Administration policies. The two groups are in many ways radically different—immigrants come here of their own volition to start new lives in a new land whereas refugees are forced to cross borders by conditions that are beyond their control. Both groups have been targeted by Trump's actions, which also target undocumented immigrants residing here—many of whom have been living and working and paying taxes in this country for decades.

A refugee from Benin in West Africa who is now a naturalized citizen, Ouro-Agoro holds seminars on how to apply for US citizenship under a program called the New Americans Initiative. She tells me that since Trump's proposed Executive Order: "There's real anxiety among the Hispanic people who come to my seminars. Many have been living here for years and they all want to become citizens. Right now."

One Human Family QCA is a group similar to QCAIR based in Davenport, Iowa. Hosted by Rabbi Henry Karp of Temple Emanuel, One Human Family QCA (a local branch of a national organization based in Key West) has reached out to disparate individuals and institutions throughout the Quad Cities with the aim of making immigrants and refugees feel welcome in their new home. Operating under One Human Family QCA's umbrella is their Immigration Task Force.

Loxi Hopkins, an Immigration Task Force member who also works as CCHD Diocesan Director for the Diocese of Davenport, tells me: "The level of fear among undocumented immigrants in the Quad Cities is quite high."

President Trump's promise to deport all undocumented workers sent shockwaves through the Latin community. In response, the

Immigration Task Force is circulating a "Blue Packet" for potential victims of Trump's proposed roundup.

Fourteen pages in length, the opening section of the Blue Packet is titled: "Precautions". It offers kernels of advice such as "provide your complete correct name" when stopped by someone from law enforcement, and stresses that one should carry all relevant documents on one's person, such as state ID, work permit, etc., and warns that possession of false documents is a serious crime.

The "Blue Packet" counsels a potential deportee not to answer questions from a law enforcement official without the presence of a lawyer and not to sign anything relating to immigration. It also recommends contacting an immigration attorney, and continues in this vein to cover such things as naming an individual to manage one's affairs in case of one's sudden and unexpected absence and includes numerous other common-sense suggestions that would chill the average American.

One Immigration Task Force member tells me: "When I give the Blue Packet to someone it's like telling them you have a terminal disease. In other words, time get your ducks in a row because you won't be around here much longer".

Araceli Masterson is a volunteer at the Palomares Social Justice Center in the Floracientes neighborhood of Moline, Illinois and a professor at Augustana College in Rock Island, Illinois, where she teaches Latin American Studies and Spanish. "People here are terrified," she tells me, describing the majority Hispanic neighborhood. "Everyone knows someone who is in danger of being deported."

She reminds me that President Obama accelerated deportations far beyond the numbers generated by any prior occupant of the Oval Office. "Undocumented workers are ready-made scapegoats. They're a reservoir of human beings to be exploited economically in low-paying jobs and when anything goes wrong in society, they're the first to be blamed. Trump has been very effective in equating immigrants with criminality."

Immigration law, she tells me, is "unbelievably complex. About forty percent of Mexican immigrants have only a primary education, but even for educated people the legal obstacles are stressful. Families have spent thousands to get a green card, have exhausted their life savings trying to get one."

Dan Vondra, an immigration attorney based in Iowa City, Iowa agrees: "It's just about impossible to get a green card if you enter the country without a visa."

He tells me that typically an applicant will enter the country on a student visa or a work visa and thereafter work toward citizenship. He says it's best to have a family member already living in the country and, if working, to be in position to prove that one's job does not displace a native worker. Marriage to a legal citizen is yet another way to get one, and there is also the controversial option of paying $500,000—presidential son-in-law Jared Kushner was recently reported attempting to sell such visas in China.

"Green cards," says Araceli Masterson, "have been taken away for any number of reasons. The protection they offer is very limited."

Dan Vondra tells me green cards can be revoked for possession of an illegal substance beyond a certain amount, for burglary or fraud or multiple DOI's. "Any sort of felony means revocation," he tells me. "Shoplifting is considered a crime of moral turpitude—loss of a green card is automatic."

If someone possessing a green card leaves the US, he or she cannot remain outside the country for more than a year. Further, re-entry to the United States can be refused for any number of reasons. "If a minor marijuana bust shows up on your record," says Vondra, "an immigration officer can deny you re-entry." Jody Mashek, an immigration attorney attached to the American Friends Service Committee in Des Moines, Iowa, tells me she's heard reports that Customs Officers are "going rogue."

The threat of deportation haunts the Latin community. Obama was known as the deporter in chief, but according to Dan Vondra, George W. Bush was in some ways even worse. "Under Bush," says Vondra, "ICE (Immigration and Customs Enforcement) agents would pick suspects up for jaywalking. For fishing without a license."

But Obama's heritage cannot be overstated. According to Jody Mashek, "Obama deported more people than all the presidents in the twentieth century combined."

Things have not improved. Under Trump, Mashek says: "ICE now has a no holds barred attitude." In the Quad Cities area there have been no mass arrests similar to those conducted in Los Angeles or New York. According to Loxie Hopkins, "ICE is arresting individuals, often in small rural towns."

In a USA Today article dated May 17, 2017, Alan Gomez writes that immigration arrests have risen 38% nationwide. "Between January 22 and April 29," he reports, "ICE arrested 10,845 people whose immigration violations were the only marks on their record. That's nearly triple the 4,242 people arrested during the same time period in President Barack Obama's final year in office." Some 45% of those presently facing deportation have never committed a crime.

Their heightened vulnerability has prompted Araceli Masterson and her staffers at Palomares to school Latin neighbors at risk not to call attention to themselves by playing loud music or having a car parked in their yard, or by leaving their kids unattended. When driving they must always use seatbelts and obey the rules of the road.

She tells me: "It used to be that a seventy-five-year-old woman who's been in this country for decades but never had proper documentation wouldn't have to worry. The authorities used to concentrate on those with criminal records, not workers who have been paying taxes for years and never broke the law. But with Trump, everyone is in the same boat."

Those at risk must make arrangements for someone to pick up their children from school, should they not return home from their job or from a trip to the grocery store, and to assure that house payments and car payments and insurance payments continue to be made in a timely fashion. One community organizer counsels the vulnerable to make out a power of attorney for property and a similar power of attorney to provide for childcare.

Araceli Masterson points out that most undocumented immigrants in the US are Chinese. In Chicago there are uncounted Polish and Irish immigrants who lack proper papers. "But no one sees them," she says. "There is definitely a racial element at work here. The term 'illegal' is reserved exclusively for those of Latin extraction. To call someone 'illegal' is to brand them an outlaw—to declare them beyond the protection of the law."

Since the election of Trump, those lacking documentation fear signing documents or showing up for community meetings. Loxie Hopkins of the Diocese of Davenport confirmed to me that attendance at mass as suffered—Hispanic church-goers are staying home. Thousands who reside in the Quad Cities area now fear being seen in public.

This fear has other consequences. Araceli Masterson at Palomares is concerned that incidents of domestic violence now go unreported, as does abuse by landlords and countless other legal abrogations that those potentially targeted for deportation don't dare address lest they be noticed by the authorities.

This fear is not unwarranted. Aracelia Masterson tells me that those who draw the attention of the police or end up in custody are far more likely to be snared by ICE. Her assertion is confirmed by statistics released by the Transactional Records Access Clearinghouse (TRAC) at Syracuse University which show that in 2015 (the most recent year for such data) 7 inmates of Mexican origin held in the Rock Island County Jail were transferred to ICE. These statistics also show that nationally 67% of all such detainees transferred to ICE are of Mexican origin.

ICE has offices at 211 19th Street in Rock Island, Illinois and at 3351 Square D Dr. SW in Cedar Rapids, Iowa. Those facing deportation in Iowa are tried before the Immigration Court in Omaha. Those arrested in Illinois are tried in Chicago.

Detainees who retain legal counsel have a far greater chance of a successful outcome at Immigration Court than those lacking such representation. There are no court-appointed attorneys for individuals charged with immigration violations, and lawyers are expensive. Palomares is organizing a fund to help defray these costs; many of those potentially targeted for deportation would otherwise lack the financial wherewithal to mount an adequate legal defense.

Becoming artful at not being noticed remains the best strategy for undocumented workers, but this tactic may no longer be adequate. In a May 18, 2017 article published by *The Detroit News* titled "Feds Use Anti-terror Tool to Hunt the Undocumented" Robert Snell reports that "Federal investigators are using a cellphone snooping device designed for counter-terrorism to hunt undocumented immigrants amid President Donald Trump's immigration crackdown, according to federal court records obtained by *The Detroit News*."

The technology at issue is a cell-site or cell tower simulator. Snell writes: "Cell-site simulators, in general, are suitcase-sized contraptions that can be installed in cars or planes to track nearby phones." One such device was used by ICE to track down and arrest an undocumented worker in the Detroit area.

In this regard, undocumented workers serve as proverbial canaries in the coal mine for the rest of us, for what is being used today to track down the most vulnerable members of the community will ultimately be wielded against everyone else.

> "While most foreign-born terrorists
> were in the country legally, ... illegal
> aliens have also taken part in almost
> every major terrorist attack on
> American soil."

Sanctuary Cities Allow Terrorists to Enter the United States Easily

Steven A. Camarota

In the following viewpoint, Steven A. Camarota argues that protecting America's national security is dependent on the mundane work of careful issuance of visas, developing a system to track the arrival and departure of foreign citizens, painstakingly verifying green-card applications and, most importantly, prosecuting those who violate the law. The September 11th terrorist attacks brought criticism on many federal agencies for their perceived laxness in security, especially for the immigration officials. However, despite the fact that these attacks were carried out by foreign-born terrorists who were in the country legally, the author states that terrorists are entering the country in many different ways. Some have even been naturalized US citizens. Steven A. Camarota is director of research of the Center for Immigration Studies.

"How the Terrorists Get In," by Steven A. Camarota, Center for Immigration Studies, September 1, 2002. Reprinted by permission.

As you read, consider the following questions:

1. What criticisms did some national agencies face after September 11th?
2. What are some of the ways that immigrants can enter the US illegally?
3. Are all terrorists illegal or undocumented immigrants?

I n the aftermath of September 11, a host of federal agencies have come under intense scrutiny. The Federal Aviation Administration, the Federal Bureau of Investigation, and the Central Intelligence Agency have all been charged with responsibility for failures leading up to the attacks. In each case, the culture within the agency, as well as its mission, policies, and procedures, has been examined in a variety of public forums. The Immigration and Naturalization Service (INS) has also been excoriated for several spectacular gaffs - most infamously, for sending notification to a Florida flight school that two of the hijackers had been approved as students six months after their deaths. But there has been no comparable effort to examine the failures of our immigration system. For example, all of the September 11 hijackers were issued visas, but there have been no extensive congressional hearings or investigations by the General Accounting Office or the Office of the Inspector General to determine whether the State Department, which issued the visas, erred in any way.

Given the fact that the current terrorist threat to the United States comes primarily from foreign-born individuals, immigration services would seem to be an obvious area of inquiry. Of course, no immigration system can be completely foolproof, but it does not have to be. Even if only some of those individuals can be detained by our immigration system, it is possible that whatever conspiracy they are part of could be uncovered.

While they were the most destructive in American history, the attacks of last September were not the first carried out by foreign terrorists on U.S. soil. To gain a more complete picture of the threat and of the holes in our immigration system, we must examine acts of terrorism in this country over the last decade. Including the September 11 hijackers, 48 foreign-born militant Islamic terrorists have been charged, or convicted, or have admitted their involvement in terrorism within the United States between 1993 and 2001. In addition to September 11, the plots examined here include the murder of employees outside of CIA headquarters in 1993, the first attack on the World Trade Center in the same year, a plot to bomb the Brooklyn subway system in 1997, plots to bomb New York City landmarks in 1993, and the Millennium plot to bomb Los Angeles International Airport. Almost all of them have now been linked in some way to Osama bin Laden's al Qaeda organization. To be sure, other terrorist threats exist. However, because the threat it poses dwarfs that of any other terrorist group, foreign or domestic, the emphasis here will be on al Qaeda.

Entering Every Which Way

In the wake of September 11, some observers have emphasized the mismanagement of temporary visas, such as those issued to students and tourists, because all of the 19 hijackers were originally allowed into the country on temporary visas. Others have argued that there is a problem with illegal immigration, because at least three of the hijackers—four if Zacarias Moussaoui, who the U.S. government claims was the intended twentieth hijacker, is included —had overstayed their visas and were illegal aliens at the time of the attacks. But in fact the danger cannot be isolated to one type of immigration. Foreign-born Islamic terrorists have used almost every conceivable means of entering the country over the last decade. They have come as students, tourists, and business visitors. They have also been lawful permanent residents (LPRs) and naturalized U.S. citizens. They have sneaked across the border illegally, arrived as stowaways on ships, used false passports, or been granted amnesty. Terrorists have even exploited America's humanitarian tradition of welcoming those seeking asylum. At the time they committed their crimes, 16 of the 48 terrorists considered in this analysis were on temporary visas (primarily tourist visas); another 17 were lawful permanent residents or naturalized U.S. citizens; 12 were illegal aliens; and 3 of the 48 had applications for asylum pending.

Even some government officials have mistakenly singled out one type of immigration as the source of the problem. During testimony before the immigration subcommittee in the Senate shortly after the September attacks, INS commissioner James Ziglar stated, "Immigrants are not terrorists.... The people that we are talking about, the hijackers, they weren't immigrants. They were nonimmigrants." While it is certainly true that the September 11 hijackers entered the country using nonimmigrant visas (also called temporary visas), the commissioner is incorrect if his comments were meant to indicate that permanent residents are not a source of terrorism. In fact, prior to September 11, most foreign terrorists were LPRs or nationalized U.S. citizens. Excluding the hijackers, more than half (17 out of 28) of the foreign-born Islamic terrorists in the last decade were persons living legally in the United States as permanent residents or as naturalized citizens.

Indeed, some of the worst foreign terrorists have been naturalized citizens. For example, El Sayyid Nosair, who assassinated Rabbi Meir Kahane in 1990, was one of the first militant Islamic terrorists to strike in the United States. A naturalized U.S. citizen, he was later convicted as a member of the larger conspiracy to bomb landmarks around New York City. Nidal Ayyad, a chemical engineer who provided the explosive expertise for the first World Trade Center bombing in 1993, was also a naturalized U.S. citizen. So too were Egyptian-born Ali Mohammed, who is widely regarded as having written al Qaeda's terrorist handbook, and Khalid Abu al Dahab, who has been described as "a one-man communications hub" for shuttling money and fake passports to terrorists around the world from his California apartment.

Lawful permanent residents (also known as green-card holders) have also played an integral role in terrorism. In all, 11 LPRs have been convicted or pled guilty to terrorist activities. These include Mahmud Abouhalima, one of the leaders of the first World Trade Center bombing, who became a legal resident after falsely claiming to be an agricultural worker, allowing him to qualify for a green card as part of the 1986 amnesty. Another LPR was Mohammed Saleh, who provided the money and the fuel oil needed to create the bombs for the massive terrorist plot targeting landmarks around New York City in the summer of 1993. The ringleader of this plot, Siddig Ibrahim Siddig Ali, was also a legal permanent resident.

The nation's humanitarian tradition of offering refuge to those fleeing persecution has also been exploited by a number of terrorists. Three of them had asylum claims pending when they committed their crimes. Sheik Omar Abdel Rahman used an asylum application to prevent his deportation to Egypt after all other means of remaining in the country had failed. Rahman inspired both the first World Trade Center attack and the plot to bomb New York City landmarks. Moreover, he is widely considered to be one of the spiritual leaders whose ideas helped to found al Qaeda. Mir Aimal Kansi, who murdered two CIA employees in 1993, and Ramzi Yousef, who was sentenced to death for masterminding the first attack on the World Trade Center, both had applications for political asylum pending.

While most foreign-born terrorists were in the country legally, either as temporary visitors, lawful permanent residents, or naturalized citizens, illegal aliens have also taken part in almost every major terrorist attack on American soil, including the first attack on the World Trade Center, the Millennium plot, the plot to bomb the Brooklyn subway system, and the attacks of September 11. Of the 48 Islamic terrorists in the last decade, 12 were in the country illegally when they committed their crimes. (It may also be more accurate to include asylum applicants in the category of illegal aliens, because all of the three terrorists discussed above had no legal basis for being in the United States and were awaiting the outcome of the asylum process.) Altogether, 19 foreign terrorists over the last decade were either illegal aliens at the time they engaged in terrorism or had lived in the United States illegally for an extended period before they committed their crimes.

How did all these terrorists get into the country? The plain fact is that they exploited weaknesses in nearly every part of the U.S. immigration system, from its visa-processing operations overseas, to control of the border and ports of entry, to green-card issuance. An examination of these problems reveals inadequate vetting of visa applicants, lack of cooperation among U.S. agencies and between the United States and foreign governments, failure to adequately police the borders, and a complete lack of interior enforcement.

Eyes Wide Shut

In a very real sense, Foreign Service officers are America's other border patrol. It is they who determine, in most cases, who is allowed into the country. Of the 48 terrorists considered here, 41 had at some point been approved for a visa by an American consulate overseas. Though we cannot expect that in every case the visa-processing system will quickly identify the terrorist applicant and prevent him from getting a visa, the fact that so many terrorists made it through certainly suggests that there are significant problems in the system.

The primary tool used in flagging terrorists is called the "watch list" or "lookout" system. It is a compilation of several million people who are not to be issued visas or otherwise allowed to enter the country. Currently, the database is composed of names, dates of birth, countries, and passport numbers rather than biometric identifiers such as photographs or fingerprints. The names of persons applying for visas are checked against the list. In some cases, procedural failures and outdated technology have caused the system to fail.

Probably the most infamous person to be mistakenly issued a visa is Egypt-born Sheik Omar Abdel Rahman. Although on the watch list, Rahman was issued a tourist visa because consular employees in Khartoum, Sudan, did not properly check the list. Although most large corporations had computerized their databases by the mid 1980s, most consular offices were still using microfiche to store and search names on the watch list. This made it much more likely that a name could be missed. Similarly, Ali Mohammed was placed on the watch list in 1984 but was still able to get a visa from an American embassy in Cairo. The list was not automated at the time, and his extremely common name may account for the oversight. Mohammed eventually married an American and lived in the United States for many years, working for al Qaeda and helping to plan a number of attacks. Learning the names of al Qaeda terrorists is an enormous intelligence challenge, but in the cases of Sheik Rahman and Ali Mohammed, whose links to terrorism were known, the system should have kept them from entering the country.

However, not all problems were the result of INS or State Department failures. In a number of cases, it appears that U.S. intelligence agencies or foreign governments did not inform the INS or the State Department that an individual might be a security risk.

Mahmud Abouhalima and Zacarias Moussaoui were both known to U.S.-friendly governments as individuals with links to terrorism. As a teenager in Egypt, Mahmud Abouhalima became involved with the outlawed al-Jama'a Islamiyya, an Islamic extremist organization. He had been under surveillance by the Egyptian government, and a number of his associates were imprisoned prior to his 1981 departure for Germany. But because his name was not on the watch list, Abouhalima was granted a tourist visa in 1985 by an American consulate in Germany. Zacarias Moussaoui's circumstances were similar. Moussaoui was known as a possible terrorist to French authorities, but his name was not on the U.S. watch list. And because France is part of the visa waiver program, which allows people to enter the United States and stay for up to 90 days without a visa, Moussaoui, a French citizen, was able to enter the United States easily.

For years the State Department and the INS have complained that the intelligence agencies and FBI have not been entirely forthcoming with the names of suspected terrorists, partly because they fear sources might be compromised. The case of Khalid al Midhar, who may have piloted American Airlines Flight 77 into the Pentagon, demonstrates the importance of information sharing. Al Midhar's terrorist activities were not known to U.S. authorities when he received his business visa in Saudi Arabia in 1999 or when he entered the country for the first time in January 2000. In January 2001, while al Midhar was out of the country, the CIA became aware that he was involved in the attack on the USS Cole the year before. However, his name was not placed on the watch list until August 2001. Unfortunately, he had already re-entered the United States in July. The fact that it took the CIA several months to put al Midhar's name on the watch list indicates that, at the very least, the agency considered the list a low priority. It must be pointed out that al Midhar's visa allowed for multiple re-entries. However, if his name had been on the watch list, an INS inspector at the port of entry might have detained him.

Welcome to America

While failure to update or administer the watch list properly is clearly a serious weakness in the immigration system, the way visas are processed overseas presents an even larger problem. Before Assistant Secretary of State Mary Ryan was forced out of office last July, the Consular Service had adopted a culture of service rather than skepticism, one in which visa officers are expected to consider applicants as their customers. Satisfying the customer - the foreign visa applicant - has become one of the service's most important goals, leading to pressure to speed processing and approve marginal applications. As one former Foreign Service officer has written, "State Department procedures call for supervisory review of refusals, but not issuances - thus, relatively inexperienced junior officers are trusted to issue visas but are second-guessed on refusals." Visa officers are judged by the number of applications processed each day and by their politeness to applicants rather than on their thoroughness in screening applicants.

The case of Lafi Khalil, who was involved in the plot to bomb a Brooklyn subway station in 1997, illustrates a number of problems with the way interviews are conducted overseas. In November 1996, Khalil received a transit visa from the U.S. Consulate in Jerusalem for travel through the United States to Ecuador. A subsequent investigation found that Khalil had been interviewed only briefly by a consular officer, and that the officer did not require him to produce a plane ticket for Ecuador nor to demonstrate that he had funds for the trip. The officer also did not consider requiring him to catch a connecting flight in "transit without visa" status, which would have required him to stay in the airport.

Khalil appears never to have had any intention of going to Ecuador. After he cleared immigration inspection, he boarded a flight to Syracuse, New York, and remained in the United States until his arrest in July 1997. Clearly, this would not have been possible had the consular officer attempted to verify Khalil's story or simply not granted him a transit visa.

While some terrorists received inadequate interviews, others never had any contact with a consular officer. At least three of the September 11 hijackers (Abdulaziz Alomari, Salem al Hamzi, and Khalid al Midhar) obtained their visas through a system called "Visa Express" used by the American consulates in Saudi Arabia, which allows applicants to submit their applications and supporting documents through a designated travel agency. Although the applications are reviewed at the consulate and the names are run through the watch list, the applicants are never interviewed by a consular officer. Without having an in-person interview, the issuing officer cannot be sure that the person applying for the visa is actually the person named in the submitted documents and application. All varieties of deception and fraud become much more difficult to detect.

The Visa Express system was set up to make things easier for Saudi Arabian applicants and to reduce the workload of the consulate. But such a system is completely inappropriate for a country like Saudia Arabia where, as was known even prior to September 11, a large share of the population was sympathetic to bin Laden's ideology.

Give Me Your Terrorists

Inadequate or absent interviews have also rendered Section 214(b) of the Immigration and Nationality Act a much less effective tool for keeping out terrorists. Section 214(b) states that individuals who appear likely to overstay their temporary visas and try to settle permanently in the United States are not to be issued one. An applicant is supposed to demonstrate that he has a residence abroad to which he is likely to return, that his visit to the United States will be temporary, and that he has enough money to finance the visit and return trip.

Officers are trained to look for evidence of strong ties to the applicant's home country, such as family, a good job, and property, and to be skeptical of an applicant who fits the profile of someone who will overstay his visa. The criteria vary from country to country, but suspect individuals are generally young, unemployed or earning a low income, and unmarried. Individuals who apply outside of their countries of nationality should invite additional scrutiny, according to consular regulations and training manuals. Often these applicants are the ones who have difficulty establishing ties to their home country or to the country in which they now live.

Though designed to prevent illegal immigration, Section 214(b) also offers protection against the terrorist threat. Persons with families, property, and other commitments in their home countries are less likely to be part of a terrorist plot, especially one that involves suicide. Moreover, many senior members of Islamic extremist movements live outside of their own countries (often in the West) because the security services in most Muslim countries have crippled their organizations at home. Sadly, the provisions of Section 214(b) have been only weakly and sporadically enforced.

A number of the September 11 hijackers almost certainly should have been refused a temporary visa under Section 214(b). Ringleader Mohammed Atta was single, unemployed, and had lived in Germany and not his home country of Egypt for most of the 1990s. It is hard to see how he could have overcome the mandatory presumption that he would likely overstay the tourist visa he was issued. It appears that at least three other September 11 hijackers, those who provided the muscle to overpower the flight crews, should also have been denied visas under 214(b). Hijackers Mohand al Shehri, Majed Moqed, and Ahmed al Haznawi were all reportedly in their early twenties, unmarried, and had little income. The September 11 hijackers are not the only militant Islamic terrorists who should have been classified as individuals likely to overstay their visas. Mohammed Salameh, who was involved in the plot to bomb New York City landmarks, was given a tourist visa in 1988, despite the fact that he was only 19 years old, unmarried, and reportedly making $50 a month in Jordan.

By Land or By Sea

Lax border enforcement have also facilitated the entry of al Qaeda terrorists. The nation's ports of entry are the places where people traveling by land, sea, or air legally enter the United States. These entry points are staffed by immigration and customs inspectors. Of the 48 terrorists considered here, 45 of them had contact with an inspector at a port of entry.

In some instances, inspectors have succeeded in preventing terrorists from coming into the country. The Millennium plot was averted when Ahmed Ressam was stopped by an inspector at the border - the officer thought Ressam looked nervous. And Ahmad Ajaj was placed in detention when an inspector at JFK airport realized he was trying to enter the country on a fake Swedish passport - although he still took part in planning the first World Trade Center attack from his jail cell. These cases show why careful inspection at the port of entry is critical to homeland security.

"Good" Policy is Actually Bad Policy

Sanctuary policies are laws, ordinances, resolutions, executive actions, or any initiatives that prohibit local officials from inquiring, acting on, or reporting an individual's immigration status—even when there is reasonable suspicion that an individual is in the country illegally. Many sanctuary policies restrict law enforcement agencies from cooperating with federal immigration officials, including prohibiting their compliance with immigration detainers. The U.S. is currently home to more than 300 sanctuary jurisdictions.

According to U.S. Immigration and Customs Enforcement estimates, roughly 2.1 million criminal aliens are living in the U.S., over 1.9 million of which are removable. These criminal aliens continue to live in communities and engage in further criminal activity when state and local law enforcement are prohibited from cooperating with federal immigration officials.

Illegal immigration is a huge burden to state and local governments, costing taxpayers an estimated $113 billion in 2013. A majority of this expense – $84 billion – is borne by state and local taxpayers. These costs come in the form of educational, healthcare, welfare, and law enforcement expenditures to illegal aliens and their families. By giving them a place to live and work where they can go undetected, sanctuary policies encourage further illegal immigration that only serves to increase these costs.Tolerating illegal immigration and providing a "safe haven" for illegal aliens is unfair to immigrants who respect our nation's laws. In addition to waiting months or years to come here, legal immigrants abide by the entry, employment, health, and processing laws and regulations set by our government. Besides giving future prospective immigrants little incentive to follow the law, sanctuary policies are an affront to those who do it the right way.

What can state and local lawmakers do to address sanctuary policies in their communities?

- Enact legislation to prohibit sanctuary policies.
- Restrict funding to jurisdictions that ignore the law.
- Require state and local cooperation with federal authorities.
- Grant victims of sanctuary policies a voice by allowing them to sue the responsible entity.

"'Sanctuary' Policy Is Bad Public Policy," Federation for American Immigration Reform, June 2016.

While such inspections have caught a few terrorists, the main tool used for identifying terrorists is still the watch list, to which inspectors at ports of entry have access through the Integrated Border Information System administered by the Customs Service. However, the names of people entering the country are often not checked against the list because of time constraints, limited personnel, and computer problems. At the Canadian border, most people crossing through are not checked against the list.

Since individuals entering under the visa waiver program have never had their names checked by an American consulate, it is crucial to do so at the port of entry. Still, some have asked why a person with a visa, who has been cleared by a consulate, should have his name checked each time he enters the United States. But as the case of September 11 hijacker Khalid al Midhar shows, an individual can be identified as a terrorist after he receives his visa but before he enters the country. For the system to be effective, the names of all persons entering the country must be checked against the list. There is no technological impediment to checking all names at all ports of entry, though doing so would require far more resources, including computer equipment, training, and personnel.

Inadequate computer systems, staffing, and training at ports of entry have also made it difficult to record arrivals and departures from the United States. Congress did pass legislation in 1996 to create an entry-exit database. But because of INS incompetence and significant opposition from the business community, the project went nowhere. As a result, the INS does not know whether foreign visitors admitted on temporary visas actually leave the country when their visas expire. There is no mechanism for tracking land departures, and the system for tracking arrivals and departures by air, which is how most visa holders travel, is largely nonfunctioning. The current practice requires foreign visitors to fill out a two-part form with their names, passport numbers, and destinations. The opportunities for failure are enormous: Airlines often neglect to collect the forms on outbound flights or forward them to the INS;

visitors may enter by air but leave by land, leaving no trace of their departure; and the information on the paper forms may be illegible or be improperly keyed into the system by the INS contractor.

Obviously, time limits on a visitor's stay in the United States are only meaningful if we can determine whether the deadline has been honored. At least 13 of the 48 terrorists from the last decade overstayed a temporary visa at some point prior to taking part in terrorist activities. Had we had a functioning entry-exit system, we could have developed policies to go after those who overstayed their visas, perhaps disrupting one or more terrorist attacks over the last 10 years. The establishment of an entry-exit system is envisioned in recently passed legislation, but it remains to be seen whether it will ever be implemented.

Terrorists have also slipped into the country illegally. Several have sneaked into the country at our sea ports. Millennium conspirators Abdelghani Meskini and Abdel Hakim Tizegha both originally entered the United States as stowaways on ships that docked at a U.S. port. Crew members of cargo ships, stowaways, and those being smuggled into the country are all potential threats. Other terrorists have entered the country from Canada. After originally coming as a stowaway, Tizegha eventually went to Canada for a time before slipping back across the northern border. Gazi Ibrahim Abu Mezer (who planned to bomb the Brooklyn subway system) also tried to sneak across the Canadian border. Tizegha was captured only after he successfully entered the country and took part in the Millennium plot. Mezer, on the other hand, was caught three times between 1996 and 1997 trying to sneak into the United States. A Palestinian, Mezer had been turned down for a student visa in 1993 at the American consulate in Jerusalem. Yet he eventually received a Canadian student visa. On his third attempt to enter the United States illegally in June 1997, the Canadian government refused to take him back. The INS then paroled him into the United States and started deportation proceedings against him. If we improve our visa processing system but fail to strengthen our land borders, we can expect more cases like these.

The fact that the INS released Mezer into the United States points to anther deficiency - a lack of detention space for holding aliens arrested for violations of immigration law or whose asylum claims are being adjudicated. While the INS does contract space from local jails, at present the agency does not have enough funding to hold most aliens who are in deportation proceedings or who have asylum claims pending. This longstanding problem has allowed terrorists to remain at large in the United States. Ramzi Yousef did not have a valid visa when he arrived at JFK airport in September of 1992, but he applied for asylum and was paroled into the United States while his claim was adjudicated.

Mir Aimal Kansi, the murderer of two CIA employees in 1993, overstayed a business visa and later applied for asylum. Instead of being detained, he was issued a work permit for a year while his asylum claim was pending. (As part of reforms implemented in 1995, the INS no longer automatically issues work permits to asylum applicants.) As detailed above, attempted New York subway bomber Gazi Ibrahim Abu Mezer was also paroled into the United States in June 1996 because of insufficient detention space. This lack of detention space effectively makes the northern border meaningless.

Homeland Security

A potential weapon in the fight against terrorism is the knowledge that many of the terrorists considered here violated America's immigration laws before taking part in terrorism. Twelve of the 48 terrorists were illegal aliens when they committed their crimes, and at least five others had lived in the country illegally at some point prior to taking part in terrorism. Moreover, at least five others had committed significant violations of immigration law prior to their terrorist acts. In addition to overstaying temporary visas and sneaking into the United States, terrorists have violated immigration laws in a number of different ways. Both Fadil Abdelgani, who took part in the plot to bomb New York City landmarks, and Khalid Abu al Dahab, who raised money and helped recruit new members for al Qaeda, engaged in fraudulent marriages to American citizens. Sheik Omar Abdel Rahman was able to obtain a green card by qualifying as a minister of religion using a false name. At least eight terrorists had held jobs for extended periods while living in the country illegally. This number includes several of those involved in the 1993 World Trade Center attack, the plot to bomb New York landmarks, and the Millennium plot.

The current immigration system has many points of weakness. It does not vigorously interview or carefully check the backgrounds of visa applicants. Nor does it enforce time limits on temporary visas. Fraudulent applications for green cards are often approved, and people in the country illegally are allowed to work, open bank accounts, and receive driver's licenses. The INS and consular officers are simply overwhelmed by the number of applicants they must process, and are stretched so thin that they cannot do their jobs. In addition, the nation's borders remain largely undefended. No system, of course, will catch every terrorist every time, but a more tightly controlled immigration system would greatly increase the chances that at least some of those involved in a large conspiracy like the September 11 attacks will be caught.

For our immigration system to be an effective part in the war against Islamic extremists, it does not have to become an antiterrorist operation. With the exception of improving the watch list, most of the problems identified above involve the mundane work of careful issuance of visas, developing a system to track the arrival and departure of foreign citizens, painstakingly verifying green-card applications and, most importantly, prosecuting those who violate the law. Failure to learn from past mistakes and to develop a better, more thorough immigration system will significantly increase the chance of another attack on American soil.

*"President Donald Trump signed
an executive order that threatened
to strip federal aid to 'sanctuary
cities' that he says fail to enforce
the country's immigration policies.
In Massachusetts, two of the state's
poorest cities have filed a lawsuit
challenging the executive order."*

Cities That Are Terrorist Targets Still Welcome Immigrants

Elizabeth Ross

*In the following viewpoint, Elizabeth Ross contends that US cities
that are most vulnerable to terrorist attacks nonetheless offer
sanctuary to immigrants. Two cities in Massachusetts—Lawrence
and Chelsea—have filed a lawsuit against Present Trump's executive
order on immigration. The author describes these two cities and
their immigrant populations, and indicates that the lawsuits could
provide a path for other cities to also challenge the order on the
grounds of unconstitutionality and other legal issues. Elizabeth Ross
is a producer for PRI's The Takeaway.*

"How Can 'Sanctuary Cities' Resist Trump? This Lawsuit Could Provide A Blueprint," by
Elizabeth Ross, The Takeaway, April 6, 2017. Reprinted by permission from PRI®.

As you read, consider the following questions:

1. How does the Lawrence, Massachusetts, lawsuit create a "blueprint" for sanctuary cities?
2. Why will Lawrence suffer if President Trump pulls federal funding?
3. Why is the population of immigrants in Lawrence so large?

E arlier this year, President Donald Trump signed an executive order that threatened to strip federal aid to "sanctuary cities" that he says fail to enforce the country's immigration policies. In Massachusetts, two of the state's poorest cities—Lawrence and Chelsea—have filed a lawsuit challenging the executive order.

This legal action could offer a blueprint for other small communities looking to push back on President Trump's immigration agenda. On April 10, the Trump administration responded by filing a motion to dismiss the complaint.

Lawrence is an urban, industrial city some 25 miles north of Boston. Waves of different immigrant groups have flocked to the city since the mid-1800s to work in the towering red-brick textile mills that still line the winding Merrimack River. The mills have long been shuttered, and the city is still trying to get back on its feet, but immigrants have not stopped coming to Lawrence. These days, three-quarters of the city's residents are Latino or Hispanic, and more than 37 percent were born outside the United States.

English language classes are especially popular in Lawrence. Thousands of residents are on waiting lists hoping to attend English as a second language programs like the ones at the Greater Lawrence Community Action Council. Executive Director Evelyn Friedman says the classes are invaluable.

"Many of our students come and they have no English language skills, and they're working at very menial jobs and as they gain skills they move up in their organizations or are able to get better jobs,"

Friedman says. "The other thing is that they can't communicate with the teachers of their children."

Lawrence could lose out big time if President Trump is able to follow through on his threat and pulls the city's federal funding. Almost 30 percent of the population in Lawrence lives in poverty and the city relies heavily on federal aid, receiving more than $36 million each year, which is about 13 percent of its annual budget. The federal money helps support ESL classes and many basic services, including the city's public schools and its free lunch programs.

Lawrence Mayor Dan Rivera is the son of a single immigrant mother who once worked in the Lawrence mills. Growing up, Rivera says he benefited personally from many federally funded programs and calls himself a "poster boy for all the good stuff that government can do."

"I'm a public school kid, a public higher education kid," he says. The GI bill helped him buy his first house, Rivera explains. "My mom was on food stamps, [and] we did public housing."

Like most sanctuary cities, Lawrence police will hand over criminals to Immigration and Customs Enforcement, but will not help ICE with civil immigration investigations and detentions, the way the president wants them to. Supporters of Lawrence's policy claim it is a matter of public safety and that it encourages all residents, even those who are undocumented, to cooperate with local law enforcement.

The mayor also says his cash-strapped police force does not have the resources to help more, even if he wanted them to.

"I got 80,000 people here ... [and] I gotta fight a drug war. I gotta fight homelessness problems and an opioid problem. I got to have police officers to go respond to car accidents," he says. "And to be punished, for not having that resource, it's basically an unfunded mandate."

Lawrence and the city of Chelsea are trying to block Trump's executive order and have filed a lawsuit that argues they are not violating any federal immigration laws with their policing policies. It also calls the executive order unconstitutional. Rachel Rosenbloom, an immigration law professor at Northeastern University, agrees.

"So, the question is: Does the federal government have the right to withhold funds from sanctuary cities? Can the president cut off funds without Congress? I think that the answer to that is no," Rosenbloom says.

While Congress can attach some restrictions to federal programs, there are limits, according to Rosenbloom, and it cannot, as the Supreme Court has put it, hold a gun to a state's head.

"If Congress wants to have a particular program that it funds and it creates some strings that are attached that are specifically for that program, that's pretty common," Rosenbloom says. "But if Congress uses unrelated funds and says, 'We won't give you these funds unless you carry out immigration enforcement actions,' the Supreme Court has said in other cases, that is not permissible under the Constitution."

Iván Espinoza-Madrigal, the executive director of the Lawyers' Committee for Civil Rights and Economic Justice, which, along with the Goodwin law firm, helped Lawrence and Chelsea file their federal lawsuit, says he hopes "that other communities in other states will be able to replicate the blueprint that we have created here and create a mix of civil rights, community-based and sanctuary communities that all come together to speak with one voice." He wants them to challenge what he calls Trump's "anti-immigrant agenda."

The Trump administration has not yet responded to Lawrence and Chelsea's lawsuit. Under the rules of the federal court in Boston, it has until next week to do so.

Periodical and Internet Sources Bibliography

The following articles have been selected to supplement the diverse views presented in this chapter.

Ryan Ahari, "Trump's actions undermine his 'protect the homeland' objective." The Hill, December 30, 2017. http://thehill.com/opinion/national-security/366792-trumps-actions-undermine-his-protect-the-homeland-objective

Michael W. Cutler, "Sanctuary Cities Endanger National Security and Public Safety." The Social Contract Press, Volume 26, Number 2 (Winter 2016). http://www.thesocialcontract.com/artman2/publish/tsc_26_2/tsc_26_2_cutler.shtml

Stephen Dubois, "Sessions: 'Sanctuary cities' undermine law's moral authority." Chicago Tribune, September 19, 2017. http://www.chicagotribune.com/news/nationworld/politics/ct-sessions-sanctuary-cities-20170919-story.html

Anna Giaritelli, "ICE threatens 'at-large arrests' after California passes sanctuary city law." Washington Examiner, October 6, 2017. http://www.washingtonexaminer.com/ice-threatens-at-large-arrests-after-california-passes-sanctuary-city-law/article/2636773

Matthew Green, "How the Kate Steinle Murder Case Thrust Sanctuary Cities into the National Spotlight." KQED News, October 25, 2017. http://ww2.kqed.org/lowdown/2017/10/25/explainer-what-are-sanctuary-cities/

Kevin Johnson, "Attorney General Jeff Sessions: Sanctuary cities 'undermine' gang fight." USA Today, April 18, 2017. https://www.usatoday.com/story/news/politics/2017/04/18/attorney-general-jeff-sessions-sanctuary-cities-undermine-gang-fight/100602066/

"Sanctuary Cities and National Security." Security Degree Hub. Accessed January 4, 2018. https://www.securitydegreehub.com/sanctuary-cities/

"Sanctuary City Toolkit." National Immigration Law Center, June 26, 2017. https://www.nilc.org/issues/immigration-enforcement/sanctuary-city-toolkit/

"Statement on Sanctuary Cities Ruling." The White House, April 25, 2017. https://www.whitehouse.gov/briefings-statements/statement-sanctuary-cities-ruling/

Do Sanctuary Cities Help to Maintain Democracy?

Chapter Preface

The United States has, throughout its history, sought to spread the idea of democracy through the world, with the idea that democracy helps promote international peace and stability as well as helping the US in general achieve security and prosperity. In both the United States and the European Union, one of the important democratic values is that of humanitarianism: the belief in the value of human life. This value of caring for other people and trying to help them is part of what fuels the sanctuary cities movement. Not only does a sanctuary city demonstrate the value of the lives of immigrants, especially those who have escaped persecution and violence in their homelands, but also shows that communities come together to govern themselves and share equally in caring and working together, which helps maintain democracy. In fact, advocates argue that sanctuary cities themselves are an invention of democracy and democratic values. It can also be said that sanctuary cities give immigrants the opportunity to see democracy in action, in the institutions and everyday lives of American citizens. They also argue that orders and legislation that ban sanctuary cities are actually working against democracy, depriving citizens not only of their right to make community decisions, but ultimately also depriving some members of society of basic public services like healthcare, housing, and education, when these programs are defunded as part of "punishing" sanctuary cities.

However, opponents of sanctuary cities could claim that President Trump's executive order is reflective of what the majority of Americans want, as indicated by his election as president, which is democracy in action. Others even say that sanctuary cities are by definition unconstitutional, which also goes against the founding democratic principles of the United States. Looking at the ideal of the United States having a responsibility to spread democracy throughout the world, sanctuary cities could be considered as a tool used toward this goal. But it can also be viewed as a threat to democracy and the stability of the United States itself.

> *"Many wonder if disobeying the president will merely cost them funds for law enforcement. Or will it also cut money for critical programs, including education, clean water and public housing?"*

Executive Orders Banning Sanctuary Cities Work Against Democracy

David Trilling

In the following viewpoint David Trilling examines the many communities struggling to understand the executive order that promises to punish sanctuary cities. Many feel that the threat of cutting federal funding to these communities is not only a threat to the health and well-being of their citizens, but also a threat to basic democratic principles as well. Several Supreme Court rulings suggest that the federal government cannot link immigration to funding for unrelated programs, but many sanctuary cities are still preparing for a fight to continue the funding for programs that are essential to their populations. David Trilling is a staff writer for Jouranlist's Resource.

As you read, consider the following questions:

1. What questions do communities have about President Trump's threatened funding cuts?
2. What are some of the rumors about immigrants and crime?
3. Why would it help sanctuary cities to argue that President Trump's executive order is "coercive"?

Donald Trump ran for president promising to be tough on immigration. Five days after taking office, he ordered Washington to cut funding to so-called "sanctuary cities" that defy federal immigration orders.

Communities around the country are struggling to understand the order. Many wonder if disobeying the president will merely cost them funds for law enforcement. Or will it also cut money for critical programs, including education, clean water and public housing?

Typically, sanctuary jurisdictions ignore federal Immigration and Customs Enforcement (ICE) orders, such as requests to hold unauthorized immigrants — often people picked up for minor crimes who would otherwise be released — while ICE petitions a court to begin deportation proceedings. Police and prison officials in sanctuary jurisdictions sometimes also restrict the information they share with ICE.

Defenders of sanctuary policies argue that local police lack the resources to hold these people. They add that sharing information discourages interactions between immigrant communities and the police, which could undermine public safety.

Critics of sanctuary jurisdictions argue that they are too easy on suspected criminals and that they encourage people to enter the United States illegally. These critics often point to the murder of a San Francisco woman in 2015, allegedly by a man who had been deported five times and was at large because the city had not honored an ICE request to detain him.

The sanctuary debate pre-dates Trump's election by decades. Today it hinges on a number of court decisions that give municipalities broad discretion over their interaction with federal officials. Since 2015, Congress has considered, but not passed, several bills that would restrict federal funds to sanctuary jurisdictions — of which there is no precise definition and thus no exact number (maybe a few hundred).

Here we outline the legal arguments, the budget implications, and the latest non-partisan research on sanctuary cities and the president's promise to punish them.

Trump's Executive Order

"Sanctuary jurisdictions across the United States willfully violate federal law in an attempt to shield aliens from removal from the United States. These jurisdictions have caused immeasurable harm to the American people and to the very fabric of our republic," reads President Trump's January 25, 2017, executive order 13768 (EO). "[J]urisdictions that willfully refuse to comply […] are not eligible to receive federal grants, except as deemed necessary for law enforcement purposes by the Attorney General or the Secretary [of Homeland Security]."

In response, the Congressional Research Service (CRS), a non-partisan government think tank working for Congress, issued a short brief on questions raised by the EO:

- Since there is no legal definition of "sanctuary" jurisdictions, which communities are affected? (The Justice Department describes them in a 2016 memo as entities that fail to report "aliens in custody" to the federal government.)
- Does "federal law" include "any federal statute or regulation or is [it] limited to federal immigration laws"?
- The EO includes a caveat: "to the extent consistent with law." The CRS notes in another brief that "it is unclear the degree to which this reference might limit the application of funding restrictions in particular contexts."

- Finally, which federal funds are affected? In a March 2017 brief, the CRS observes that the EO gives the Attorney General and the Secretary of Homeland Security discretion to decide which grants could be withheld: "A broad interpretation of 'federal grant' could include any federal grant outlay to designated sanctuary jurisdictions regardless of which federal agency administers the grant program. A more narrow interpretation of the definition of 'federal grant' could limit the affected grant programs to those programs directly administered by the Attorney General and the Secretary" – i.e. law enforcement and border security programs funded by the Justice Department and the Department of Homeland Security (DHS).

As we discuss below, several Supreme Court rulings suggest that the federal government cannot link immigration to funding for unrelated programs. Nevertheless, some municipalities fear, and are preparing for, a fight.

Challenges

There are over 11 million unauthorized immigrants in the U.S., according to government statistics. The Pew Research Center estimates that more than half live in just 20 major metropolitan areas, such as New York, San Francisco, Chicago and Boston.

As the essence of Trump's plan became clear after his election victory, cities began vowing to resist. The mayor of Somerville, Massachusetts, for example, issued a defiant statement in November 2016 declaring his Boston suburb a "sanctuary city."

> How much federal funding could we lose? A lot. Currently Somerville receives approximately $6 million in recurring federal funds per year for things like special education, school lunch programs, substance abuse prevention, and homeland security. That constitutes about 3 percent of our annual budget. Additional grants for programs such as housing are also sought each year. If we lose this funding, we will tighten our belts, but we will not sell our community values short.

CONSTITUTIONAL OR NOT?

For months, the Trump administration has tried to bully local communities into signing up to become extensions of the federal deportation system. That campaign of threats and public shaming based on flawed data—which has been mostly unsuccessful—suffered another major blow yesterday. A federal court in San Francisco ruled in two cases that the president's threats were unconstitutional, and stopped the government from carrying them out anywhere in the country. The ruling vindicates the constitutional rights of cities, counties, and states to refuse to participate in deportations. And like the court orders halting the president's Muslim ban, the ruling shows the crucial role that courts play in preventing presidential overreach.

In response, the president has repeatedly threatened to punish localities that decline to join his proposed deportation force. Just days after being sworn in, he sought to make good on those threats, signing an executive order threatening to defund jurisdictions that do not agree to participate in immigration enforcement. San Francisco and Santa Clara County, with support from the ACLU and others, sued. As they explained in court papers, their sanctuary policies placed them squarely in the administration's crosshairs. The threats to strip them of federal funding were having devastating effects on their budgeting processes, and, they argued, violated the Constitution.

The court agreed. It refused to accept the government's assurances that it would take only a few grants from sanctuary cities, explaining that the government's narrow interpretation rendered the executive order an "ominous, misleading, and ultimately toothless threat," inconsistent with the order's text and the administration's public statements.

The court then explained that the executive order was unconstitutional in a number of ways.

The principles underlying the court's decision are constitutional bedrock. The Constitution divides power between the federal government and the states, and among the three branches of the federal government, to ensure that no single person or government will ever have the power to eliminate the rights and freedoms we all cherish. Those values were vindicated by the ruling yesterday.

"Federal Court Calls Trump's Threats to Defund Sanctuary Cities Unconstitutional," by Cody Wofsy, ACLU, April 26, 2017.

After Trump's EO, residents of the neighboring town of Arlington – population roughly 43,000 – began debating whether to declare their community a sanctuary. In a fact sheet, town authorities say that of the last 1,000 criminal arrests (over an unspecified period), "only one had an immigration detainer, and in this instance, federal officials chose not to pursue it." The town receives no federal police funding, but it does collect roughly $4.5 million in federal grants annually (about 3 percent of its budget) for education and low-income residents. The fact sheet acknowledges that the Trump administration could try to cut these funding sources.

Washington D.C., stands to lose up to 25 percent of its budget if the EO is applied, according to a *Washington Post* calculation that estimates New York City could lose 9 percent.

A January 2017 Reuters analysis found the nation's 10 largest cities could lose $2.27 billion annually in federal funds if the executive order succeeds: "Among the funds at risk are $460 million that the federal government gave out to fund Head Start pre-school programs in the 10 largest 'sanctuary cities' in the most recent fiscal year, the analysis found. Washington also sent $238 million to municipalities to fund airport improvements and $153 million for HIV prevention and relief."

Within days of the EO, several cities had filed lawsuits challenging it as unconstitutional, including Chelsea and Lawrence, Massachusetts, and San Francisco, arguing that the order violates the Fifth Amendment for being vague and the Tenth Amendment for "commandeering" a local government.

The National Conference of State Legislators has detailed several of the arguments communities could use if they defy or sue the Trump administration:

- A 1987 Supreme Court ruling (*Dakota v. Dole*) limited Congress's ability to set conditions that are not "germane" or "related to" the purpose of a federal grant. Withholding education spending, for example, is unlikely to qualify as germane to an immigration order.

- Cities could also argue that the EO is "coercive." The Supreme Court ruled coercion unconstitutional in 2012 when it struck down the Medicaid expansion provision of President Obama's health care law, arguing that forcing states to accept the expansion in order to receive federal funding amounted to a "gun to the head." That would, many have argued, violate Congress's Constitutional spending powers.
- The Supreme Court has interpreted the 10th Amendment, which defines states' rights, to prohibit the federal government from "commandeering" state powers or requiring state or local governments "to enact or administer a federal regulatory program."

Federal Grants

If the Trump administration manages to overcome the legal obstacles to shutting off funding to sanctuary communities, most of that funding will be discretionary — assistance to states and local governments that is administered through federal agencies such as the Department of Agriculture or the Department of Housing and Urban Development (HUD). The government's Catalog of Federal Domestic Assistance describes 2,308 federal programs and provides contact information for the agencies that award the funding, which can come in the form of grants. The grants are often managed by state or local governments or other local groups.

A March 2017 report from the Congressional Research Service describes federal grants and how they are awarded. It estimates that in fiscal year 2017 grants to state and local governments exceed $596 billion. Total outlay data by program is available from the Office of Management and Budget. State and local governments often publish figures for how much they receive from each program, but so far most have been left guessing what they might lose.

- A 2014 paper in the Journal of Law and Economics investigated Secure Communities, a federal program between 2008 and 2014 that automatically transmitted arrest data to immigration authorities, who could check the immigration status of any detainee. (This is the kind of federal program that sanctuary cities oppose — refusing, for example, to hold non-violent detainees after they have been processed.) The paper found "no observable effect" on crime rates in the cities where the program was implemented.

- Another 2014 paper, this time in the journal *Criminology and Public Policy*, found a similar lack of impact on crime from the Secure Communities program. It also found that critics of the program had little reason to fear it would enable discriminatory policing.

- A 2012 paper in the Annals of the American Academy of Political and Social Science found that immigrant communities in Chicago experienced lower levels of crime than average; in Los Angeles, these communities were prone to higher levels of crime. The authors speculate that characteristics specific to Los Angeles may help explain why it is an outlier. The article begins with a review of studies showing that neighborhoods with high numbers of immigrants experience lower-than-average crime levels in general.

- A forthcoming paper by scholars at Highline College and the University of California Riverside found no association between sanctuary jurisdictions and rates of violent crime or property crime.

> "*The President's plans to deny federal funds to hundreds of cities, counties, and states will do nothing to solve our immigration problems.*"

Cities and States Can't Fix Our Immigration Problem

Nathan Kasai and Sarah Trumble

In the following viewpoint Nathan Kasai and Sarah Trumble argue that sanctuary cities contribute to democracy. The issue of sanctuary cities has been a point of political tensions since President Trump's executive order in January of 2017. However, many people do not have a clear definition of just what these cities are, what President Trump wants to do about them, and what specifically any punishments for these cities would entail. Nathan Kasai is Policy Advisor for Third Way, a Washington think tank. Sarah Trumble is Deputy Director of Social Policy and Politics for Third Way.

As you read, consider the following questions:

1. According to this article, what would punishing sanctuary cities actually mean?
2. Why is it so difficult to define sanctuary cities?
3. What is President Trump's strategy for getting rid of sanctuary cities?

"What You Should Know About Sanctuary Cities," by Nathan Kasai and Sarah Trumble, Third Way, March 2, 2017. Reprinted by permission.

W hile sanctuary cities have become a point of political tension in recent elections and on Capitol Hill, the issue isn't as black or white—or as red or blue—as it may appear at first glance. Cities across the country, in both Democratic and Republican states, have expressed unwillingness to take on immigration enforcement as a direct result of decades of Congressional failure to pass comprehensive reform. According to the *New York Times*, there are five states and 633 counties that could be considered "sanctuary cities" by some definitions of that term. And tens of millions of people live in these areas. This includes not only large liberal cities like Los Angeles, New York, and Chicago, but also cities like Tucson, AZ, and Tuskegee, AL, and even counties in states like Georgia, Iowa, Kansas, Kentucky, Nebraska, North Dakota, and Wyoming.

President Trump's recent executive order attempts to make good on his campaign promise to crack down on sanctuary cities by denying them federal funds. In this memo we examine what sanctuary cities really are, what Trump and his allies are attempting to do to punish them, and what those actions would really mean for their communities.

What Exactly Is a Sanctuary City?

Despite the ubiquitous use of the term "sanctuary city," it has no clear legal definition. Immigration hardliners tend to define it as a jurisdiction that is acting in violation of federal immigration law, but that's actually very rarely the case. A more expansive use of the term might refer to those jurisdictions that do not fully cooperate or assist in federal immigration enforcement efforts, often while still acting in full compliance with federal law. In practice, they don't even need to be "cities" per se. Sanctuary cities can be cities, counties, states, and even local jurisdictions that offer certain services to immigrants (like providing an attorney for people facing deportation proceedings) or refrain from arresting a person based solely on their immigration status.

One of the most common sanctuary city practices is to deny federal Immigration and Customs Enforcement (ICE) requests to detain immigrants for extra time after they have completed a jail sentence. When a person is arrested and booked in a local or county jail, their fingerprints are sent to the FBI. The FBI then shares this information with ICE, who checks the individual's immigration status—regardless of where they were arrested. If this check shows that the person is undocumented, ICE can detain the person once they have served their sentence so long as it has a warrant. If it doesn't have a warrant, it can issue a "detainer request" asking the local jail to hold the person mostly on the jail's dime for an additional 48 hours while it attempts to obtain one. All compliance with detainer requests from ICE are—and must be—voluntary for local jurisdictions because federal courts have held that holding someone without a warrant or probable cause in these circumstances violates the Fourth Amendment of the Constitution. More and more courts are also ruling that complying with a detainer request by holding an individual for extra time itself violates the Fourth Amendment and that cities are liable for any harm suffered by that extra detention.

Detainer requests don't just cause constitutional issues for cities, they also create a significant financial burden on local law enforcement agencies. In New York City, the cost of detaining an inmate is about $460 dollars per day. It's $145 in Chicago, and $129 in Los Angeles. The federal government's reimbursements for detaining an immigrant on their behalf fall drastically short of these costs. In 2016, the average daily detention reimbursement by ICE to local cities was $47.10 per day. New York City alone was reimbursed about $10 million from the federal government in 2016 for holding immigrants. When it's considered that New York City is only reimbursed for about 10% of its daily detention costs, it becomes clear that American cities are spending hundreds of millions of local tax dollars to detain immigrants for the federal government.

Given these challenges, sanctuary cities respond to detainer requests in a variety of ways—some accept detainer requests where the individual has prior felony convictions, gang ties, or is on the terrorist watch list, some remind ICE as the person's release date approaches but won't agree to hold them after their sentence has been completed, and some accept detainer requests but won't house an immigrant throughout the entire deportation process. But all must adhere to existing federal law requiring they communicate with ICE about who is in their custody and when they will be released. And even where a jurisdiction will not comply with detainer requests, the immigrants in their custody still must face any criminal charges on which they were booked and serve out whatever jail sentence a judge hands down if they broke the law. And if ICE shows up to get someone when he or she is released, local officials cannot stop them.

What Does President Trump Want to do About Sanctuary Cities?

President Trump, joined by immigration hardliners in Congress, has promised to "get rid of" sanctuary cities by defunding them and cutting off access to new federal funding streams. One of President Trump's first executive orders blamed sanctuary cities for causing "immeasurable harm to the American people and to the very fabric of our Republic," and multiple defunding bills have been introduced by his allies on Capitol Hill.

President Trump's executive order directs the Secretary of Homeland Security to officially designate "sanctuary jurisdictions," requires the Administration to "ensure that…sanctuary jurisdictions are not eligible to receive Federal grants," and authorizes the Attorney General to take "appropriate enforcement action" against them. Though the order first defines sanctuary cities as only those failing to comply with federal reporting requirements— which virtually none do—it also refers to any entity that "has in effect a statute, policy, or practice that prevents or hinders the enforcement of Federal law"—which could easily be read to apply to jurisdictions that choose not accept every ICE detainer request to hold immigrants longer than their sentence. However, because Congress typically sets the eligibility requirements for federal grants, the President can't unilaterally or retroactively change them. That makes it unclear how much funding could actually be withheld on the President's authority alone.

In Congress, those supportive of a Trump-style immigration crackdown have introduced several pieces of legislation targeting sanctuary cities in recent years. These proposals provide a much more explicit picture of what defunding could look like, and they generally target either federal development grants or law enforcement grants. Congressional plans to withhold federal funds to sanctuary cities include:

- The No Sanctuary for Criminals Act (115th Congress): Sponsored by Representative Bob Goodlatte (R-VA), the bill prevents cities from limiting their compliance or cooperation with federal immigration authorities "in any way," effectively compelling them to accept all detainer requests. Those that don't would become ineligible for any law enforcement grants from the Department of Justice or Department of Homeland Security, as well as for their grants related to terrorism, national security, immigration, or naturalization.
- The Stop Dangerous Sanctuary Cities Act (115th Congress): Sponsored by Senator Pat Toomey (R-PA), the bill would deny grants from the Department of Housing and Urban Development to any sanctuary city. These grants total hundreds of billions of dollars annually and help cities expand and improve infrastructure.
- The Enforce the Law for Sanctuary Cities Act (114th Congress): Sponsored by Representative Duncan Hunter (R-CA), the bill would withhold Department of Justice law enforcement assistance grants to any city that refuses to notify ICE when they arrest an undocumented immigrant (which cities are already legally prohibited from doing).

- The Mobilizing Against Sanctuary Cities Act (115th Congress): Sponsored by Representative Lou Barletta (R-PA), it would prevent cities from receiving "federal financial assistance," including any grant, loan, property, or insurance, for a one-year period if the Attorney General declares them a sanctuary city.
- The No Transportation Funds for Sanctuary Cities Act (115th Congress): Sponsored by Representative Jason Smith (R- MO), the bill would deny Transportation Investment Generating Economic Recovery (TIGER) grants to any city that refuses to hold undocumented immigrants until DHS can transfer them to federal custody. TIGER grants account for roughly $500 million annually. Chicago alone received $25 million in 2016 from this program.

What Would Punishing Sanctuary Cities Actually Mean?

Cracking down on sanctuary jurisdictions is harder than it looks—and not only because the label is extremely difficult to define. Constitutional principles of federalism dictate that the federal government cannot "hold a gun to the head" of states financially—which means that when the federal government offers money to the states, it has to be actually voluntary for states to accept it. The money can't be so important or so much of the state's budget that the state is left with no choice but to take the money and comply with the federal demands. Moreover, when the federal government denies funding to a state, the reason for denying the funding has to be related to the funding. The federal government for example, can't deny education dollars to punish a state for polluting too much. Nor can the federal government commandeer state and local officials to do its own bidding. It's the right and responsibility of each state to control their own public servants—the federal government cannot barge into a state and tell them what their own state and local police forces must do. But there are some things the President or Congress could do to punish cities and states they consider to be sanctuary jurisdictions that could possibly survive judicial review:

Cutting off Discretionary Executive Agency Funding

President Trump could use his presidential authority to deny cities funds whose distribution is at the discretion of federal agency heads. This could include funding streams for equipment for first responders, sewer and water grants from the Environmental Protection Agency, or transportation infrastructure support. Cutting off this money likely would not be enough to pressure states or cities into submission, though—these discretionary federal grants alone simply don't make up enough of a state or city's budget to be coercive. As such, it is nearly certain that President Trump would need Congressional action to really make cities feel it in their wallets.

Denying Access to Future Congressionally-allocated Development Funds

In 2015, the federal government provided roughly $630 billion in grant money to state and local governments. Community Development Block grants (CDB) —a program targeted in some of the previous defunding bills—distributed about $3.26 billion in grants to states and cities in 2016 alone. Going forward, Congress could predicate eligibility for these funds on cooperation with all ICE activities. This action would cut off sanctuary cities from federal development funding that allows communities to create affordable housing, fund legal assistance services, and open food banks. Denying sanctuary cities access to this money would make life more difficult for low- and moderate-income families and hurt city development efforts—including in some of the country's largest and most economically important cities. Philadelphia, for example, received roughly $47 million from 2014-2015 in CDB grants. The city of Los Angeles (not including the county or surrounding cities in the metropolitan area) received $52 million. And New York City received $203 million. On the campaign trail, President Trump frequently vowed to "fix" and "rebuild" America's inner cities, which he called a "disaster." But cutting off access to millions of dollars' worth of federal affordable housing grants won't "bring hope and opportunity to our inner cities" like he promised—in fact, it would hurt the very communities he professes to want to help.

Reducing Law Enforcement Funding

Another popular target of defunding proposals are law enforcement funds—especially Department of Justice grants to state and local police forces. These formulations would prohibit designated cities from receiving State Criminal Alien Assistance Program (SCAAP) funding—which reimburses state and local law enforcement agencies for incarcerating immigrants convicted of felonies or multiple misdemeanors—as well as Department of Justice (DOJ) law enforcement grants. DOJ grants totaled roughly $3.5 billion in 2016 and allowed local police departments to acquire needed equipment. The grants also help provide training programs on issues like de-escalation, active shooter response, and prisoner reentry. Houston, Texas for example, received a roughly $750,000 grant in 2016 to combat human trafficking. And Charlotte, North Carolina received $1.25 million for sexual assault kits. DOJ grants are vital in expanding local police professionalism and capacity, and withholding these dollars won't make communities safer or do anything to improve our immigration system.

Conclusion

Efforts to punish sanctuary cities don't just come with fiscal consequences. Law enforcement officers across the country have found that they are most effective and that their communities are safer when residents trust the police and believe that they can turn to them when in need. That may explain why sanctuary cities actually have lower crime rates than other jurisdictions.

The President's plans to deny federal funds to hundreds of cities, counties, and states will do nothing to solve our immigration problems. Nor will it improve city infrastructure, make urban-dwellers safer, or help President Trump deliver on his campaign promises to make cities great again. Local police forces have limited resources, and they shouldn't be punished for prioritizing serious crime prevention over immigration enforcement. Immigration policy is the responsibility of the federal government. And cities and states cannot fix our broken immigration system. Only Congress can do that, and its failure to act means that cities will continue to have to muddle along until federal policymakers step up and take on their responsibility.

"These dollars go to everybody. You cut these grants—these are grants that protect the whole population."

Losing Federal Funding Can Adversely Affect Residents of Sanctuary Cities

Shefali Luthra

In the following viewpoint, Shefali Luthra sheds a light on the damage done to all residents of sanctuary cities whose funding is threatened. Trump's executive order would affect immigrants and programs aimed at assisting them, but it could also harm the citizens of these cities who rely on federal programs for health care, housing assistance, efforts to combat opioid addiction, and domestic violence programs, as well as other federally funded programs. This is forcing local officials to plan for potential defunding, often resulting in a reduction of services. Shefali Luthra is a Kaiser Web reporting fellow.

As you read, consider the following questions:

1. What programs will be most affected by losing federal funding?
2. Why is it so hard to tell which cities will be affected?
3. What are some of the strategies used by city that are at odds with the federal government's policies?

"Trump's Vow To Squeeze 'Sanctuary Cities' Could Play Havoc With Health Programs," by Shefali Luthra, Kaiser Family Foundation, May 1, 2017. Reprinted by permission.

The Trump administration's tough stance on immigration has some local health department officials worried it could spur cuts in federal funding and complicate a wide variety of programs, from efforts to battle the opioid epidemic to domestic violence initiatives.

The Department of Justice (DOJ) sent letters April 21 to nine jurisdictions—including the state of California and cities such as Chicago, New Orleans, Philadelphia and New York—threatening to deny them agency funding because of their status as "sanctuary cities." That federal assistance broadly supports criminal justice initiatives, but it often reaches well beyond police departments and courtrooms to include violence prevention programs and other efforts to address social factors that affect health.

"These dollars go to everybody. You cut these grants—these are grants that protect the whole population," said Dr. Georges Benjamin, executive director of the American Public Health Association.

This KHN story also ran in *Governing* magazine. It can be republished for free (details).

Local health officials also worry that other federal agencies may follow Justice in stringently implementing a controversial Jan. 25 executive order signed by President Donald Trump that mandates federal agencies take action to ensure localities comply with federal immigration laws and help deport people in the country illegally. That order—which has been blocked temporarily by a federal judge—could jeopardize a broad swath of vital community health services, not only for undocumented immigrants but for legal residents and citizens, too.

Rhetoric Vs. Reality

The term "sanctuary cities" describes locales—cities, but also states, counties and other community entities—with policies known as "separation ordinances," which separate local government responsibilities from those of federal immigration authorities.

They often direct local police officers not to ask about the immigration status of victims, witnesses or suspects unless it is directly relevant to the case. They also exempt local law enforcement from complying with detainment or notification requests from the Immigration and Customs Enforcement (ICE) agency. In some circumstances, the local or state agencies declare that they won't meet requirements to ask about immigration status when people apply for benefits.

Officials from these jurisdictions say helping federal authorities detain someone—especially if that person turns out to have valid documentation—could be a violation of due process. The officials say that if they comply, they could be at a legal risk. They also argue that enforcing some of the federal directives is a waste of resources or could deter immigrants from reporting crimes or assisting in investigations because they are afraid of police.

But there is no hard-and-fast definition of "sanctuary cities" or federal delineation of which jurisdictions would be targeted under Justice Department directive.

"There's been a lot of rhetoric around sanctuary cities," said Laura Vazquez, a senior legislative analyst at the National Council of La Raza, a Latino advocacy group. "That has resulted in cities being confused. ... They're concerned if their city is losing funding."

And health officials are already wary.

"The DOJ has been excellent partners before for many of our efforts," said Dr. Leana Wen, Baltimore's health commissioner. "It would have a negative impact if we were to lose any federal funds."

What's at risk? Take the opioid epidemic. DOJ has worked hand in hand with the Department of Health and Human Services to spearhead the federal government's response—and allocates millions of dollars to local agencies for activities like prescription drug monitoring, helping people access the most effective models of treatment and equipping police officers with anti-overdose medications.

"This is a big problem. It gets worse if you don't have the resources to address it," Benjamin said.

In Baltimore, Wen said, the impact would likely be felt by the city's Safe Streets program, a health department initiative meant to undermine gang violence with an emphasis on curbing shootings. The federal department has over the years put millions of dollars toward it, enabling public health officials to work with schools, local churches, community organizations and other groups. And, depending on the jurisdiction, other public health interventions could also be squeezed: domestic violence response programs, drug courts and mental health courts, among other things.

There's also a lack of clarity about which cities might be affected. New Orleans, for instance, doesn't self-identify as a sanctuary city but received the letter from Justice. The source of its scrutiny: Police officers don't routinely question witnesses or victims about immigration status, said Zach Butterworth, the city's director of federal relations. He argued the city's policies are consistent with federal law and have been vetted by legal authorities.

A cut in federal funds would be a setback, said Marsha Broussard, who directs the city's health department. Ironically, she added, the city's programs supported by Justice mostly benefit legal residents, since New Orleans has a fairly small undocumented population.

Legal Uncertainty, And A Broad Impact

Though the idea of losing the Justice grants causes concern, health department heads said the bigger worry is that other federal agencies will follow suit. Losing federal support from HHS, the Department of Housing and Urban Development and others could jeopardize activities ranging from HIV treatment, family planning services and Zika preparedness to routine immunization outreach and screening homes for lead.

"Obviously it wouldn't be good, and it would hamstring our efforts" to lose those funds, said James Garrow, a spokesman for Philadelphia's public health department.

San Francisco—whose health department received at least $68 million in federal funding—filed suit in January seeking relief from Trump's executive order, arguing the funding ban is unconstitutional. A federal judge in the city issued a preliminary injunction on Tuesday. The Trump administration has indicated it will appeal.

Other legal challenges are pending in Richmond, Calif., the Massachusetts towns of Chelsea and Lawrence, and Seattle. There's also interest in Portland, Ore., and New York City. Their legal argument: The sanctuary cities directive is unduly coercive.

In addition, the New York attorney general has issued a legal guidance arguing the Trump administration lacks authority to stop "sanctuary" policies. That has encouraged some municipalities to adopt strategies at odds with the federal stance, such as not asking people about their immigration status and not enforcing civil warrants from ICE.

The legal uncertainty makes it harder for health programs planning around what federal defunding might mean in practical terms. And, until then, Benjamin said, they might have to scale back.

"If I'm not sure about a grant that's coming, and I'm not sure I can hire people, I'm not going to spend the money," he said. "The money may not be legally tied up, but you are, financially."

Locally, that matters, Wen said.

"We are on the front lines. We are the ones safeguarding health and wellness of our cities every day," she said. "Having our residents suffer is not an option."

> "It has always been an important matter for the health and well being of the United States to integrate ethnic and other national cultural affinities with the psychology, attachment, and cultural affinities of the American national community."

Immigrants Are Central to America's National Community

Stanley Renshon

In the following excerpted viewpoint, Stanley Renshon argues that emotional attachment to the American national community is the foundation of the United States, and the success of American democracy and its cultural and political institutions has always depended on these kinds of emotional connections. Debate among Americans about immigration is not a new thing. Part of the debate is about how to create attachment for immigrants, through language and acculturation, to help them develop an American identity. Stanley Renshon is professor of political science and coordinator of the Interdisciplinary Program in the Psychology of Social and Political behavior at the City University of New York Graduate Center.

"Becoming American: The Hidden Core of the Immigration Debate," by Stanley Renshon, Center for Immigration Studies, January 1, 2007. Reprinted by permission.

As you read, consider the following questions:

1. What three critical developments helped build the immigration debate?
2. What is America's central, core immigration issue, according to the author?
3. What do both liberals and conservatives agree is the thing that unites Americans?

America has begun a long-delayed and contentious national immigration debate that has been building for over a decade. It has been stimulated by the confluence of three critical national developments: the terrorist attacks of 9/11 that destroyed the comforting assumption that "it can't happen here" while underscoring American vulnerability caused in part by an easily exploited immigration control system; the unprecedented numbers of new immigrants from diverse cultural and political traditions that have raised important questions about this country's capacity to integrate them into the American national community, how best to do so, and immigrants' interest in doing so; and the increasing awareness that the issue of illegal immigration represents not only a national security challenge but also a challenge to the very fabric and nature of American democratic life.

The new immigration debate has been crystallized by the Bush administration's guest-worker program proposal that would "regularize" the status of millions of illegal immigrants already here, and provide a framework for their eventual citizenship. That, and similar proposals like the McCain-Kennedy bill, have sparked fierce debate. The Republican Party is split between those who do not want to reward illegal immigrants with an amnesty for their violation of American immigration laws and those who see an economic benefit from the labor of immigrant workers. The Democratic Party is eagerly anticipating the prospect of adding eight to 10 million new illegal immigrants/citizens to their voting rolls and have criticized any plan that does not include allowing most or all of the illegal immigrants here now to "regularize" their status and be put on the road to full citizenship. As often happens in such tense political standoffs, talk of "grand bargains" begins to emerge; in this case, 10 million illegal immigrants (and their families) become legal in exchange for as-yet-unspecified "enforcement."

"Enforcement will be the key" to any new border deal, asserts one typical news story. The new policies will be "tough as nails" promises another grand bargain advocate. Past experiences with such calming reassurances should leave skeptical anyone with even an ounce of realism. The bilingual education program that is at the center of so much difficulty in teaching immigrants English in school started out as a measure to further English, not home languages, but was derailed and hijacked as it was implemented after congressional passage. Sanctions against businesses that hired illegal immigrants, part of the 1986 Immigration Reform and Control Act (IRCA), also contained a grand bargain consisting of enforcement and legalization, but as the Manhattan Institute's Tamar Jacoby notes, "Not only on the border, but also in the workplace, enforcement of our immigration law is close to meaningless."

Moreover, IRCA stimulated more illegal immigration, as amnesties do, since the anticipation of future "status adjustments" is historically realistic and the incentives high. Why the current suggestions for a grand bargain would differ is not made clear. The current debate springs from one basic fact and one unexamined premise. According to a report on immigration policy from the Chicago Council on Foreign Relations, the only point of agreement among those who study, are affected by, or wish to change American immigration policy is that "the system is broken." The clearest and most obvious reflection of this fact is the presence of an estimated 12 million illegal immigrants living in this country and the estimated 750,000 who enter every year.

This demographic fact leads many to a premise that has yet to be tested, much less verified. It is that illegal immigrants come here primarily to work at jobs "Americans won't do." I say this is a premise because, since there has never been adequate enforcement of our immigration laws, the United States has never really tested the proposition that legal immigration, now averaging nearly one million per year, will not satisfy our economic needs. It seems highly unlikely that the United States needs eight to 10 million farm workers, construction workers, restaurant workers, or gardeners (occupations that attract many illegal immigrants), or that if we did need more of these kinds of workers, raising salaries wouldn't provide them.

While these problems ought to be enough to caution against the easy but untested claims of grand bargain advocates, I want to make a different argument here: That the focus on grand bargains that trade legalization for enforcement misses the most important part of the immigration debate entirely. The grand bargain—however much enforcement or legalization are in the final deal—fails to get to the heart of America's immigration dilemma, what remains the hidden core of the issue.

Attachment: The Hidden Core of the Immigrant Debate

What is America's central, core immigration issue? It is this: How is it possible to integrate the almost one million new legal immigrants who arrive here each year, on average, into the American national community? How do we help them to feel more at home here, while at the same time developing the emotional attachments that will truly help them think of themselves as more American than otherwise? Before the United States adds 12 million illegal immigrants and their families to our citizenship rolls, stimulates the inevitable yearly increase in illegal aliens who will wish to be strategically placed for the next "status adjustment," and adds them to the already record-breaking numbers of legal immigrants who arrive each year, it should seriously consider the "attachment gap."

That gap is the result of centrifugal forces that have buffeted emotional attachments to the American national community by immigrants and Americans alike over the past four-plus decades. Domestically, multiculturalism has sought to substitute ethnic and racial attachments for national ones, while international cosmopolitans seek to transcend what they see as narrow and suspect nationalistic connections to the American community with international ties, including encouraging new immigrant ties to their "home" countries. All of this has unfolded as America's major cultural, political, and social institutions and practices have been under relentless pressure during our decades-long culture wars.

The focus on the emotional attachment and psychological integration of both new immigrants and those who are already American citizens into the American national community is, paradoxically, both fundamental and novel. Immigration is a policy area that has been dominated by economic arguments. Do immigrants pull their own economic weight? Do they use more economic resources than they contribute? Do they depress wages for working-class Americans? The degree of emotional attachment that immigrants feel toward their new country is hardly mentioned and never measured. Instead, we rely on surrogate measures like self-reports on English language faculty (which focus on speaking, not reading or writing), education, or home ownership. Caution is merited on all these substitute measures since few like to publicly admit their language limitations, education is not synonymous with national attachment as even a casual perusal of informed punditry will reveal, and owning a house is not the same as loving your country.

The immigration debate also has had its share of hyper-charged political rhetoric. Is helping immigrants to become attached to their new country a form of racism and cultural condescension? Are people who voice any concerns about immigration policy "anti-immigrant?" Facilitating the psychological attachment of immigrants and Americans alike to their country is too important an issue to allow it to be sidetracked by baseless accusations.

The Emotional Underpinnings of American Life

Emotional attachment to the American national community is the foundation of U.S. citizenship, this country's institutions, its way of life, and, in the wake of 9/11, a matter of national security. Liberals and conservatives alike believe that a commitment to the American ideals of democracy and justice are what unites us. According to the Manhattan Institute's Tamar Jacoby, "every schoolchild knows we are a unique nation not by blood or ancestry, but by a set of shared ideas." Or again, what holds America together? "The ineluctable common core," Jacoby says, "is a set of ideas about how the American people ought to govern themselves."

The political theorist Michael Walker has argued that it is citizenship and the fact that it is easy to become an American that binds us together. It is possible, of course, to have the rights of a citizen but to feel little emotional attachment to the country that provides them. This is one reason why a "guestworker" program that allows foreign workers to focus on higher paychecks that can be sent "home," takes American immigration policy in the wrong direction. In such cases citizenship is primarily instrumental, sought for the advantages it confers. Yet a community requires more than instrumental membership and a "what's in it for me?" calculus to function and prosper. Emotional attachments provide a community with the psychological resources to weather disappointments and disagreements and to help maintain a community's resolve in the face of historic dangers. Emotional attachment and identification are the mechanisms that underlie sacrifice, empathy, and service.

Citizenship without emotional attachment is the civic equivalent of a one-night stand. The power of the American Creed itself rests on a more basic psychological foundation. That foundation is the set of emotional attachments that often are disparaged and very misunderstood. The bonding mechanisms through which "pluribus" becomes "unum" are the diverse emotional attachments that are ordinarily summarized by the term "patriotism."

Patriotism is much more complex than the adages "my country right or wrong" or "dissent is the highest form of patriotism." And, contrary to the widely misquoted and misunderstood aphorism of Samuel Johnson, patriotism is not the "last resort of scoundrels," but an absolutely essential part of emotional bonding between Americans and their country. His oft-repeated quote referred only to those who misused the public trust, not to the virtues of patriotism. Johnson's real, less reported, sentiment was that, "no man can deserve a seat in parliament who is not a patriot."

I understand patriotism or national attachment to include a warmth and affection for, an appreciation of, a justifiable but not excessive pride in, and a commitment and responsibility to the United States, its institutions, its way of life and aspirations, and its citizens. These attachments define the basis of our identification as Americans. We don't often think about it except when events like 9/11 remind us that our attachments to this country are profound and much deeper than simply believing that democracy is the best form of government. And they are much more extensive and nuanced than the caricature of lazy patriotism, summed up by the phrase "my country right or wrong."

The success of American democracy and its cultural and political institutions has always depended on these kinds of emotional connections. Yet over the past four-plus decades those attachments have been profoundly challenged, and in many ways weakened, by domestic and international developments. Within the United States, decades of cultural warfare over everything from the nature of families to civics curriculums have weakened America's primary social, political, and cultural institutions. At the same time, multiculturalism has successfully championed the primacy of racial and ethnic identities over more national attachments. Internationally, the ease of global movements of information and people have allowed immigrants and citizens alike to be in much closer touch with their "home" countries— and allowed their home countries to be more in touch with them, primarily for self-interested reasons.

New and old immigrants have understandable attachments to their countries of origin. The question is: How can the United States facilitate attachments to this country? The answer to that question does not concern new immigrants alone. These are American national community issues. Both old citizens and new immigrants have an important stake in increasing the extensiveness and depth of attachments to the American national community. And of course, the government, representing all Americans, has a critical role to play in helping to foster American national identity and attachment—a role it has so far declined to play.

If national attachments are the psychological glue that holds this country together, how is it possible to help develop and consolidate these feelings? Certainly no laws can mandate them. Nor can we halt or reverse the march of technology and international connectedness. The truth is that such feelings can only develop out of experiences that foster them. The question is whether we can help put into place experiences that do just that.

Finding points of attachment between Americans, old and new, and this country's history, institutions, and traditions so that immigrants can see how their lives and that of the country intersect provides one strong basis for emotional attachment and the development of an American identity. Government, as well as private and civic organizations at all levels, has an important, helping role to play in this process.

"You may not have heard of the
'Nullification Crisis' that President
Andrew Jackson faced in 1832.
But there are many unfortunate
similarities between it and what is
happening today on immigration."

Sanctuary Cities Are Unconstitutional

Hans A. von Spakovsky

In the following viewpoint Hans A. von Spakovsky argues that the
existence of sanctuary cities is contrary to what is laid out in the
United States Constitution. He uses the historical Nullification
Crisis of President Andrew's Jackson's presidency to illustrate what
is currently taking place with immigration, and argues why it is
unconstitutional. The author states that the courts have in large
part ignored the Constitution, federal law, and prior precedents
when ruling on sanctuary cities. Instead, they are substituting their
judgment for that of the president, and weakening the president's
executive order. Hans A. von Spakovsky is a senior legal fellow for
the Heritage Foundation.

As you read, consider the following questions:

1. What are the similarities between the Nullification Act and today's immigration issues?
2. Why does the author believe that sanctuary cities are unconstitutional?
3. Why can't states dispute immigration and tariff laws set forth by Congress?

You may not have heard of the "Nullification Crisis" that President Andrew Jackson faced in 1832. But there are many unfortunate similarities between it and what is happening today on immigration. From the unjustified obstruction of immigration law by some activist federal judges to the defiance of the federal government on sanctuary policies by governors and city mayors such as Ed Murray of Seattle, there are some interesting parallels — and lessons.

I was reminded of the Nullification Crisis recently on a tour of James Madison's home, Montpelier, which is close to the University of Virginia in Charlottesville, Virginia. One of the docents related how President Jackson had visited Madison in the midst of his reelection campaign to get his advice. This crisis was about high tariffs which, before the implementation of the income tax in 1913 through the Sixteenth Amendment, was one of the main sources of income for the federal government.

High tariff rates were resented throughout the South, particularly in South Carolina. While they benefited manufacturers in the northern states, they hurt the mostly agricultural southern states. Led by John Calhoun, South Carolina and other states asserted that they had the final authority to declare federal laws unconstitutional and thus null and void within their states. While Jackson was a moderate on tariffs and respectful of the rights states retained in our federal system, he was scornful of the nullification theory. He considered it an unconstitutional, "abominable doctrine" that "will dissolve the Union."

In 1832, the nullifiers took control of the South Carolina government and passed the infamous "Ordinance of Nullification." They expressed the same type of virulent hostility and contempt for (and defiance of) the Jackson administration and the tariff system that we are seeing today towards the Trump administration over enforcement of federal immigration law, including provisions against certain sanctuary policies. Those states and cities are pushing the same concept of nullification of federal law, although they are doing it in federal court.

As one would expect of Andrew Jackson, he reacted strongly to this threat from South Carolina, including issuing a Nullification Proclamation on Dec. 10, 1832. Nullification was "incompatible with the existence of the Union, contradicted expressly by the letter of the Constitution, unauthorized by its spirit, inconsistent with every principle on which it was founded, and destructive of the great object for which it was formed," He wrote. The crisis was resolved by a compromise bill on tariffs that Congress passed in 1833 after passing the Force Bill, which gave the president the power to use state militias and federal forces against the nullifiers.

The similarity between these events and what is happening today are eerie. While there are many areas over which the states and the federal government share responsibility — or where the Tenth Amendment gives responsibility to the states — immigration is not one of them. Section 8 of Article I gives Congress exclusive authority to "establish a uniform Rule of Naturalization," just as Section 8 gives Congress the exclusive authority to establish and collect all "Imposts and Excises" or tariffs. The states have no authority in these areas at all. They can no more dispute the immigration rules established by Congress than they could dispute the tariffs imposed by Congress back in 1832.

This makes perfect sense. Any other rule would produce chaos. Think of the enormous problems that would be caused by border states such as Texas or California deciding that they would ignore federal law and apply their own immigration rules to individuals coming across the Mexican border into the United States — or if states decided that they would impose their own tariffs on foreign goods coming into their states in addition to those imposed by the federal government. In fact, it was that kind of behavior that was restricting trade under the Articles of Confederation between states such as Virginia and Maryland that helped lead to the call for a constitutional convention.

When it comes to immigration and the entry of aliens into the U.S., Congress delegated to the president the extremely broad authority under 8 U.S.C. §1182 (f) to suspend the entry of any aliens or class of aliens into the U.S. if he believes it "would be detrimental to the interests of the United States." As five dissenting judges at the Ninth Circuit Court of Appeals recently pointed out, there are a long series of decisions by the U.S. Supreme Court upholding the authority of prior presidents under this provision and severely limiting the ability of the courts to review the president's decision.

Unfortunately, at the urging of certain states, the courts have in large part ignored the Constitution, federal law, and prior precedents. They are instead substituting their judgment for that of the president, and enjoining the president's executive order by implementing a temporary halt to entry from certain terrorist safe havens. In essence, states such as Hawaii and Washington are turning to activist federal judges to nullify the exclusive authority of the federal government over immigration and the security of our national border — and those judges are complying.

The sanctuary policies implemented by cities such as San Francisco and Seattle also seek to nullify federal immigration law and obstruct its enforcement. 8 U.S.C. §1373 prohibits states and local jurisdictions from preventing their law enforcement officials from exchanging information with federal officials on the citizenship status of individuals they have arrested or detained. The Supreme Court upheld this provision in 2012 in *Arizona v. United States.*

Quite appropriately, Attorney General Jeff Sessions has announced that he will not award any discretionary federal grants from the Justice Department to cities that violate §1373.

Seattle has filed suit, claiming that the federal government has no right to cut off its access to discretionary funding. The city also makes the meritless claims that its policy does not violate federal immigration law.

Sanctuary cities are claiming that Sessions is trying to force them to enforce federal immigration law and that the loss of federal funds would violate the holding in NFIB v. Sebelius (2012). This is the Supreme Court decision that upheld Obamacare but found that the Medicaid portion of Obamacare, which required states to significantly expand their Medicaid coverage or risk losing all Medicaid funding, violated the Spending Clause of the Constitution. The federal government was "commandeering" the states by compelling them to "enact or administer a federal regulatory program."

But Sessions is simply trying to get states to not obstruct federal enforcement. That includes abiding by the ban contained in Section 1373. Sanctuary cities are trying to prevent federal officials from finding out about criminal alien murderers, rapists, and other violent criminals that these cities would apparently rather release than have picked up and deported so they cannot further victimize Americans. Section 1373 doesn't force local law enforcement officials to notify federal officials when they detain an illegal alien; It simply says that local governments can't ban law enforcement officials from doing so.

The spurious legal argument that §1373 violates the anti-commandeering principle was raised by the City of New York in a lawsuit against the federal government only 11 days after the provision became federal law. New York also had a policy in place that forbade city officials from transmitting information on the immigration status of any individual to federal immigration authorities. In *City of New York v. U.S.* (1999), the Second Circuit Court of Appeals threw out the city's case because the federal law was constitutional and well within congressional authority on immigration.

As the court pointed out, §1373 does not compel "state and local governments to enact or administer any federal regulatory program. Nor has it affirmatively conscripted states, localities, or their employees into the federal government's service." The only thing the provision does is prohibit state and local governmental entities or officials from "directly restricting the voluntary exchange of immigration information with the INS." A contrary holding would cause chaos: "If Congress may not forbid states from outlawing even voluntary cooperation with federal programs by state and local officials, states will at times have the power to frustrate effectuation of some programs."

> We can only hope that the current nullification crisis will also be resolved once and for all when all of the lawsuits being filed by the states to prevent the enforcement of federal immigration law reach the Supreme Court.

That is clearly what is happening here: sanctuary states and cities want to "frustrate effectuation" of federal enforcement of our immigration laws. The absence of such cooperation, as the Second Circuit said, would force federal officials to "resort to legal processes in every routine or trivial matter, often a practical impossibility." This was the same type of resistance exhibited by local governments to *Brown v. Board of Education*: "a refusal by local government to cooperate until under a court order to do so."

Furthermore, refusing to award sanctuary cities funds that have to be applied for and that are entirely discretionary within the judgement of the attorney general does not come anywhere close to "commandeering" a "State's legislative or administrative apparatus for federal purposes," which was the key factor in the NFIB decision. The Supreme Court said that there is no violation of the Spending Clause "when a State has a legitimate choice whether to accept the federal conditions in exchange for federal funds."

States can make their own decisions on whether to apply for a portion of the $4.1 billion the Justice Department has available to local jurisdictions for improving their law enforcement programs. In fact, this situation raises even fewer concerns than a federal law that the Supreme Court upheld in *South Dakota v. Dole* (1987). That law provided that states would lose five percent of their federal highway funds if they did not raise the drinking age to 21. This was "relatively mild encouragement" compared to the Medicaid expansion in Obamacare, where the Court described the potential loss of all Medicaid funding as a "gun to the head."

Similarly, when it comes to sanctuary cities, the Justice Department isn't threatening the cutoff of any major entitlement funds such as Medicaid or even state highway funds. What's at stake are discretionary grants that the states may or may not decide to apply for, and which the Justice Department may or may not choose to grant.

The Nullification Crisis was resolved when South Carolina rescinded its nullification ordinance after President Jackson issued his Nullification Proclamation. We can only hope that the current nullification crisis will also be resolved once and for all when all of the lawsuits being filed by the states to prevent the enforcement of federal immigration law reach the Supreme Court.

Periodical and Internet Sources Bibliography

The following articles have been selected to supplement the diverse views presented in this chapter.

Harald Bauder, "Sanctuary Cities Like Toronto Are Democracy's Last Stand." Huffington Post, June 15, 2017. http://www. huffingtonpost.ca/harald-bauder/sanctuary-cities_b_17102376. html

Katherine Culliton-González," Sanctuary & Inclusive Democracy: The Stunning Victories of the 2017 Election Show It's Time for Meaningful Policy Change." Demos, November 9, 2017. http:// www.demos.org/blog/11/9/17/sanctuary-inclusive-democracy-stunning-victories-2017-election-show-it%E2%80%99s-time-meaningfu

Daniel Denvir, "The False Promise of Sanctuary Cities." Slate.com, February 17, 2017. http://www.slate.com/articles/news_and_politics/jurisprudence/2017/02/the_false_promise_of_sanctuary_cities.html

Heather K. Gerken and Joshua Revesz, "Progressive Federalism: A User's Guide." Democracy, Spring, No. 44. https:// democracyjournal.org/magazine/44/progressive-federalism-a-users-guide/

Ivan Light, "Sanctuary Cities and States: The Only Legal Choice." The American Institute for Progressive Democracy, Issue 31. Accessed January 4, 2018. http://www.taipd.org/node/364

Judge Andrew P. Napolitano, "Sanctuary Cities and the Rule of Law." Creators.com, August 10, 2017. https://www.creators.com/read/judge-napolitano/08/17/sanctuary-cities-and-the-rule-of-law

"Sanctuary Cities," KCET.org. Accessed January 4, 2018. https://www. kcet.org/category/sanctuary-cities

"Sanctuary City Policy Wins in New York City." The Center for Popular Democracy, December 1, 2017. https:// populardemocracy.org/blog/sanctuary-city-policy-wins-new-york-city

Amber Tong, "What Exactly Is a Sanctuary City?" Governing, July 29, 2016. http://www.governing.com/topics/public-justice-safety/gov-sanctuary-city-congress-georgia-north-carolina.html

For Further Discussion

Chapter 1
1. Do sanctuary cities have a responsibility to protect citizens, or immigrants?
2. Would you vote to make your town or city a sanctuary city? Why or why not?
3. Should sanctuary cities create guidelines for who is protected and who is not?

Chapter 2
1. Why is there so much controversy about crime rates in sanctuary cities?
2. What types of crimes should be specifically measured in sanctuary cities?
3. Why is it difficult to link undocumented or illegal immigrants and crime?

Chapter 3
1. What specifically are the fears about sanctuary cities and national security?
2. Is national security more important than providing protection to immigrants without criminal records?
3. What safeguards should sanctuary cities put in place concerning national security?

Chapter 4
1. How do sanctuary cities reflect democratic values?
2. Does the effort to suppress sanctuary cities work for or against a democratic government?
3. Should the safety of citizens in a democracy outweigh the creation of sanctuary cities?

Organizations to Contact

The editors have compiled the following list of organizations concerned with the issues debated in this book. The descriptions are derived from materials provided by the organizations. All have publications or information available for interested readers. The list was compiled on the date of publication of the present volume; the information provided here may change. Be aware that many organizations take several weeks or longer to respond to inquiries, so allow as much time as possible.

American Civil Liberties Union (ACLU)

125 Broad Street, 18th Floor
New York NY 10004
(212) 549-2500
website: www.aclu.org/

The ACLU works to defend and preserve the individual rights and liberties guaranteed by the Constitution and laws of the United States.

American Friends Service Committee

1501 Cherry Street
Philadelphia, PA 19102
(215) 241-7000
website: www.afsc.org/key-issues/issue/immigrant-rights

AFSC is a Quaker organization devoted to service, development, and peace programs throughout the world. Their work is based on the belief in the worth of every person, and faith in the power of love to overcome violence and injustice.

American Immigration Council

1331 G St. NW, Suite 200
Washington, D.C., 20005
(202) 507-7500
website: www.americanimmigrationcouncil.org/

The American Immigration Council is a nonprofit organization promoting laws, policies, and attitudes, through research and policy analysis, litigation and communications, and international exchange, that honor the US's history as a nation of immigrants.

Catholic Legal Immigration Network (CLINIC)

8757 Georgia Avenue, Suite 850
Silver Spring, MD 20910
(301) 565-4800
https://cliniclegal.org/

CLINIC promotes the dignity and protects the rights of immigrants in partnership with a dedicated network of Catholic and community legal immigration programs.

U.S. Citizenship and Immigration Services

111 Massachusetts Avenue NW
First Floor (MS 2180)
Washington, D.C. 20529-2180
(800) 375-5283
website: www.uscis.gov/

U.S. Citizenship and Immigration Services (USCIS) is the government agency that oversees lawful immigration to the United States.

Bibliography of Books

Marisa Abrajano. *White Backlash: Immigration, Race, and American Politics*. Princeton, NJ: Princeton University Press, 2017.

George J. Borjas. *We Wanted Workers: Unraveling the Immigration Narrative*. New York, NY: W.W. Norton, 2016.

Jane Bullock, George Haddow, and Damon P. Coppola. *Homeland Security, Second Edition: The Essentials*, 2nd Edition. Oxford, UK: Butterworth-Heinemann, 2017.

Aviva Chomsky. *Undocumented: How Immigration Became Illegal*. Boston, MA: Beacon Press, 2014.

Phillip Cooper. *By Order of the President: The Use and Abuse of Executive Direct Action (Studies in Government and Public Policy)*, 2nd Edition. Lawrence, KS: University Press of Kansas, 2014.

David A. Gerber. *American Immigration: A Very Short Introduction*. New York, NY: Oxford University Press, 2011.

Tom Gjelten. *A Nation of Nations: A Great American Immigration Story*. New York, NY: Simon & Schuster, 2016.

Tanya Maria Golash-Boza. *Deported: Immigrant Policing, Disposable Labor and Global Capitalism*. New York, NY: NYU Press, 2015.

Ruth Gomberg-Muñoz. *Becoming Legal: Immigration Law and Mixed-Status Families*, 1st Edition. New York, NY: Oxford University Press, 2016.

Roberto G. Gonzales. *Lives in Limbo: Undocumented and Coming of Age in America*. Berkeley, CA: University of California Press, 2015.

Nick Hunter. *Immigration* (Hot Topics). Portsmouth, NH: Heinemann, 2011.

Hiroshi Motomura. *Immigration Outside the Law*. New York, NY: Oxford University Press, 2017.

Mae M. Ngai. *Impossible Subjects: Illegal Aliens and the Making of Modern America (Politics and Society in Modern America)*. Princeton, NJ: Princeton University Press, 2014.

David Weissbrot. *Immigration Law and Procedure in a Nutshell*, 7th Edition. St Paul, MN: West Academic Publishing, 2017.

Tom K. Wong. *The Politics of Immigration: Partisanship, Demographic Change, and American National Identity*. New York, NY: Oxford University Press, 2017.

John Zmirak. *The Politically Incorrect Guide to Immigration*. Washington, DC: Regnery Publishing, 2018.

Index

DEC 2018